Creative Change

Becoming Changemakers and
seeing the heart of lasting change

Lawrence Chong

CONSULUS PRESS

MADRID | MEXICO CITY | LONDON
BUENOS AIRES | BOGOTA | SHANGHAI

Published by **Consulus Press**

In collaboration with:
LID Publishing
An imprint of LID Business Media Ltd.
LABS House, 15-19 Bloomsbury Way,
London, WC1A 2TH, UK

info@lidpublishing.com
www.lidbpublishing.com
www.consulus.com

© Consulus Pte Ltd, 2025
© LID Business Media Ltd, 2025

ISBN: 978-1-917391-71-9
ISBN: 978-1-917391-72-6 (e-book)

Cover and page design: Consulus

To every courageous Changemaker
who creatively tries each day

"They push the human race forward,
and while some may see them as the crazy ones,
we see genius, because the people who are crazy enough
to think that they can change the world,
are the ones who do."

Apple,
'Think Different' Campaign 1997

CONTENTS

"All our knowledge has its origin in our perceptions.

The eye, which is called the window of the soul, is the chief means whereby the understanding may most fully and abundantly appreciate the infinite works of nature.

Experience never errs; it is only your judgment that errs in promising itself results as are not caused by your experiments. Because, given a beginning, what follows from it must be its true consequence unless there is an impediment."

- Leonardo da Vinci
15th century artist,
Painter,
Draftsman,
Engineer,
Scientist,
Theorist,
Sculptor,
Architect,
Illegitimate son,
Misfit,
Creative Genius,
Changemaker

Seeing Change

At 1 astronomical unit from the sun, our planet is nicely situated within the habitable zone. Solar power is essential for life, so the relationship between the sun and the Earth must be perfect. If the sun were hotter, our blue planet would be uninhabitable. And if it were a tad cooler, there would be no liquid water on Earth, a requirement for life. Is this a coincidence or simply a code of life to be found?

The earlier quote is by the Renaissance Changemaker, whose life's work in art and science was shaped by learning from seeing in all situations, whether it is the forces of nature or how society functioned. His approach can be equally applied to finding the code for shaping lasting change.

Over two decades, my team and I at Consulus have worked alongside founders, leaders, and their teams, researching and implementing systems change on a global scale. We were able to journey with Changemakers in their struggles within billion-dollar companies, social enterprises, international non-profits, and governments. Trying to figure out how to shape lasting change has been my life's work.

How did Changemakers with tiny resources creatively change industries and nations? How did they inspire movements that continue their cause generations beyond them? How did a Changemaker unite a circle of trust that can lead a broader movement? I have since learned that succeeding in change is not just about doing but recognizing how Changemakers are called differently, seeing situations with a penetrating gaze and possibilities that others have not seen, and mobilizing movements to join them to shape the world.

I want to be clear about why discovering the call for changemaking matters today. The world is currently heading towards a higher probable case of intentional failure because too many leaders in power believe that they can afford to postpone change for good. This is what Ian Bremmer, the political scientist said eloquently in 2013:

"We deserve an apology because we've got a lot of smart people but we lack leadership."

This realization then led me to describe this global problem as the "Change Power Dilemma." Despite having access to the most advanced knowledge, wealth, and global power in history, we are not intentionally applying this power to bring about positive change for the planet, for peace, and for an equitable economy.

Short-term gains have taken priority over common good and too many leaders of our time believe that humanity can afford their inaction or lack of longer-term solutions. This laissez-faire attitude has to be countered by more Changemakers who think differently and are prepared to dedicate themselves to enter into different situations to change the world for the better.

The art to see change

Two years ago, in my TEDx talk: How Your Strategy Can Be Great by Design, I shared Leonardo's "saper vedere," or "having the art to see." In his time, there were many more masters of the arts than him. Since he was an illegitimate child, he was not entitled to a formal education. Yet despite this, he saw deeper and further than most people in his time; these insights enabled him to imagine new approaches and solutions creatively. This means if we choose not to be blind, we can see that the solutions and strategies are right before our eyes.

Leonardo da Vinci, like other Changemakers, was not superhuman. They simply found their cause because they cared more about the issue, so they saw deeper and further.

In understanding the world around them, they found creative ways to shape it.

In addition to the insights I gained, prior to writing this book, I invited a worldwide circle of 33 friends—each one a Changemaker in their own way—from different walks of life to share their views about what they want me to write. Their contributions have been invaluable to shaping this book so that it can be useful to anyone who is sincere in driving change. There were also hundreds of useful comments and questions following my TEDx talk that has been viewed by thousands, which I included in these pages. Over the last 15 years, I have learned much from my different interactions with my over 300,000 followers on LinkedIn. Thank you to each of you who contributed in some way to shaping this experience.

In search of creative ways of seeing solutions, my approach has been to consider a diversity of ways, going beyond business and economics, which involved learning from historic battles, upstart invaders, nation builders, religion, and culture. Like Leonardo, I am taking an approach that is open to seeing all situations. It may cause discomfort, but I see new solutions by considering as many perspectives as possible.

I want to emphasize that I did not write this book as a detached professor researching a subject matter. I am personally invested in this process since changemaking has gifted me with an adventure that allowed me to discover a bigger global family. I have been through the pain of grief and loss but have also experienced incredible joys in this journey. I have tried to capture the highs and lows of being a Changemaker in writing these pages.

My book circle asked for short stories, useful approaches, and reflections. I have taken a storytelling approach following the lives of individuals, both familiar and unknown, throughout history. I have chosen unique episodes from 'superstar' individuals who possessed an iron will and 'nameless' groups like those that challenged the Berlin Wall who, despite being initially powerless, made a courageous decision to challenge the status quo and found creative ways to bring about change.

The inclusion of some notable figures in this book does not mean that their characters are spotless. I acknowledge that they were flawed individuals just like us. I decided not to shy away from controversial characters as I focused on their impact and how they shaped the world through their actions.

Whether you are facing a crossroads in your life, staring at a mountain after you have understood your cause, leading a non-profit in an area that few care about, sitting in an office in New York pondering how your company can balance social change and be viable as a business, watching over your kids in Jakarta, or discerning how you can shape real change while you serve in the government, these 'threads' are written to help you find the journey that only you can determine. I call them threads as I hope some of these thoughts can contribute to the weaving of your change journey, and as we are all on different paths, some of us are closer to completing our search while some only needed a nudge or a confirming thread.

Amidst the chaos and confusion, being able to see change is always better than fear.

Ultimately, this book is written as a strategic playbook for the Changemaker in you who wants to make a difference. This is not a book for personal improvement or wealth accumulation. I had many drafts for this book, and earlier versions were too pleasing to appeal to everyone. But when I went to Africa, inspired by fellow Changemakers there, I decided to 'lion up' and say that change is possible for those called to shape it.

So, fellow Changemakers and Changemakers-to-be, this book is for you.

B. VISUAL MAP FOR THE PREMISE OF THE BOOK

Seeing the Heart of Creative Change

Creative Change Cycle

This is similar to a visual map that provides an overview of the different sections like if you were to be given a tour of the masterpiece that is the Sistine Chapel. For those of you who have watched my TEDx talk, I talked about a masterpiece code and this is an expanded version of that.

There is a formula in all the chaos. Based on years of research and experience, I can say that it is possible to see a way forward and I call this the "Creative Change Cycle."

At the heart of this cycle are four elements that Changemakers need to shape lasting change, which are: Cause, Creative Vision, Circle of Trust, and Competent Pivot. However, before discovering these four elements, a Changemaker needs to first be able to see things differently to continuously shape lasting change.

Every part of this book begins with a parable that frames the core principles. Each key passage from that parable is further explained through stories of Changemakers, facts, and practical frameworks for the purpose of applying them in different situations.

Let us go through this guide one step at a time.

First, imagine the world turning like a regular wheel, representing business as usual.

The first sign that a Changemaker is uniquely called towards a particular cause is that they will start to figure out the cardinal points of failures or fragility of a moment in history. Hence, the triangle represents the person's gaze extending to grasp the cardinal points of the wheel of time. This is what we will explore in Part One, Seeing With a Lion's Gaze from Threads 1 to 13.

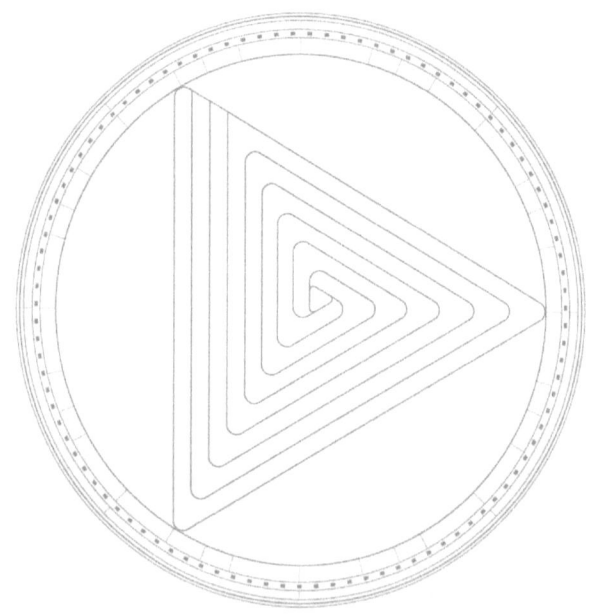

After being gifted with the capacity to see the key challenges of various situations, it now becomes important to discern carefully if this is the kind of change you are meant to bring about. So, the first test that comes to the Changemaker: Is this the cause you are called to do and to be? You will face incredible odds and you will be tested to see if this is truly your cause. This will be in Part Two, Cause: Finding Your Everest with Threads from 14 to 25.

After discovering your cause, possessing the unique ability to weave a creative vision is the confirmation that this particular journey is meant for you. The vision would be so attractive that it draws others, which is what we shall explore in Part Three, Vision: Building Your Cathedral with Threads 26 to 37.

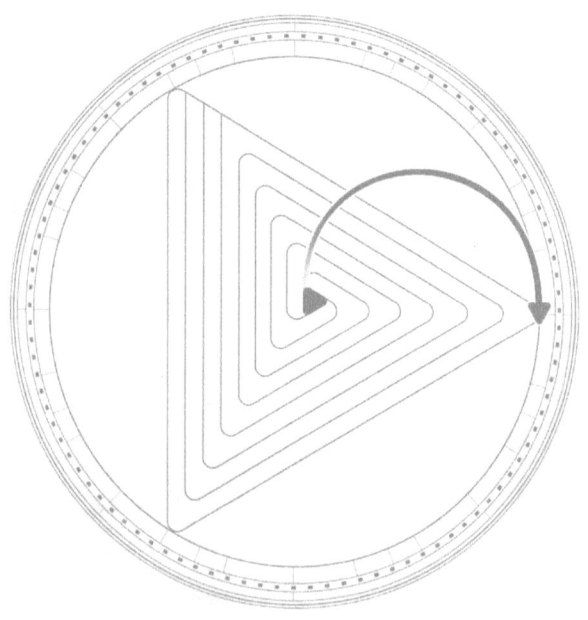

When the cause is validated with the presence of a creative vision, the next confirming sign of these two is when a core circle of trust composed of talented individuals joins your cause to build out the creative vision. This is what we will reflect on in Part Four, Gathering Your Core with Threads 38 to 50.

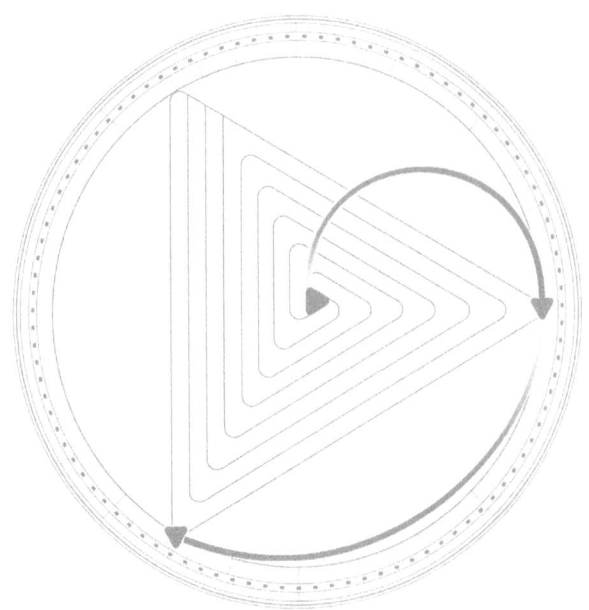

There needs to be more than a clear cause, a creative vision, and a circle of trust because having adaptable abilities and innovation to create change matters. So, if the right people are drawn and their collective ability matches with what is needed to fulfill the creative vision, these elements result in a new way of doing things, thus generating a "Creative Change Cycle" heartbeat effect. We will explore this in Part Five, Competent Pivot: Pivoting Like A Butterfly with Threads from 51 to 60.

A constant flow of energy pulsates from the cause which enriches the creative vision and expands the circles of trust while drawing relevant talent to enable creative change. The creative change effect is almost like a song that others will resonate with and want to be part of. The litmus test of lasting change is the ability to mobilize a movement to come along with your cause.

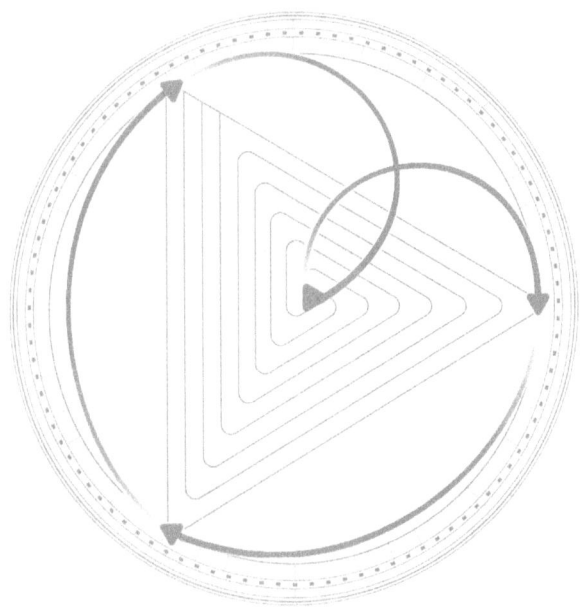

Companies that almost failed, such as Apple, eventually became a trillion-dollar juggernaut to leapfrog much larger players like Microsoft to dominate the tech industry. Meanwhile, an unlikely island nation like Singapore with no hinterland, succeeded as an economic powerhouse that even the UK, a former empire, sought to emulate its vision post-Brexit. What do both of these examples share? They succeeded because their leaders had a clear cause, vision, and were able to draw a core circle of leaders who then mobilized a movement for change. Both examples also achieved their respective transformation through creative competency.

Over time, any Creative Change Cycle's momentum will wane, so a new generation must rise to renew the vigor of the cause. In a more complex age where algorithms can shape how we think, live, work, and interact with others, we must think critically about what will happen if we keep surrendering our capacity to think on our own and what that means for our advancement as a thinking species.

Knowing where talent and money flows will determine the future in good and bad ways. Here, we will explore the possible four futures where there is much hope for progress and the idea of four horsemen that can devastate humanity if those trends become unstoppable. We will explore this in Part Six, Seeing Beyond from Threads 61 to 79.

In a time of crisis, the need for more Changemakers has become more urgent than ever. If a Changemaker finds the cause they are meant for, the effect this can have on the world would be exponential.

Every Changemaker is on a different stage in their journey. Whether you are an activist, working professional, or a leader in power, you are all called towards a worthy cause. Hence, this book is anchored on six parables to help you recall and apply the lessons that are relevant to your situation. For some of us who are certain about where we are headed, only some of these parts are needed. For others, it is about seeing the whole journey. This book is about discovering something new and seeing possible pathways for your journey.

May you learn to see with a lion's gaze, find your Everest, and build a cathedral so attractive that it captivates a core circle of kindred spirits who will journey with you to achieve creative change.

Ultimately, even though Changemakers are often told that the change they seek is impossible, they pursue it because they believe that it is possible.

At the time of publishing, no dictionary
has officially defined what a Changemaker is.
Here is my definition:

Changemaker/s:

A person or persons who have a specific cause despite the odds and is creatively changing the world for good while mobilizing a movement for lasting change.

Eye-opening Moments

Seeing

New York City, 2010

Amidst the crowds of hurried pedestrians and honking vehicles, I found myself in Union Square, East 14th Street, dressed in a windbreaker with the words "Arms Down" emblazoned in red. Holding a giant red flag with the exact same words, I, too, was a red flag shouting for attention. Just then, a policeman eyeballed me and started walking in my direction. I thought, "I must be in trouble." As a Singaporean, standing in a public square to promote a campaign to reduce global arms spending was a first for me. So, at that moment, I did not know whether I should bolt or stand still. My friends were all spread out, and they could see what was happening. "What is this campaign about?" asked the officer. I breathed a sigh of relief when I realized that he was simply curious.

I explained that my friends and I, part of Religions for Peace, the world's largest interfaith network, are gathering 20 million signatures to convince the world's governments to divert 10% of their arms spending towards meeting the Millennium Development Goals (MDGs). He listened intently and then asked, "So, if the world's governments did agree, will we have world peace? Will we stop the bad actors?" I knew I did not have good answers then, and we left it as is.

Eventually, the campaign indeed became futile. After a year of effort involving thousands of youth around the world, only one country without a military signed the pledge. Costa Rica.

Being involved in interreligious dialogue globally really opened my eyes and showed me that evil is often more intentional than good. Why do I say this? Too many of us as Changemakers believe that simply doing good is enough but the challenge is how to match the scale of those who do evil. Evil actors such as terrorists or extremists tend to do much bigger and more ambitious things, like taking over governments.

Another thing I realized is how skilled evil actors are at fundraising and how systematic they are in sowing discord. They are often way more organized than the people of goodwill. I was not deterred by the lack of success in my experience with Religions for Peace but I was determined to find a way to shape change because I discovered my calling at a younger age.

Finding Cause

Rome, 1995

To the tune of the song, "*Facciamo vedere il mondo unito,*" which means "Let us show the united world," 16,000 young people from 180 nations sang and clapped. Here at the Paleur Stadium in Rome, I am at a gathering called the Genfest—the festival for the new generation. The war in Yugoslavia was going on at that time and lively music soon gave way to pin-drop silence when youth who had lost families and friends shared their horrifying experiences at war. However, what was most impressive was how, despite the loss of hope and family, many found the strength to forgive and still believe in a united world. At its conclusion, an Italian lady, who would eventually be awarded the UNESCO Peace Prize in 1996, came to speak to us. Chiara Lubich. She told us that unity can be a sign of our times and that we should bring this idea into schools, religious communities, and companies. Then she said:

> "*Young people do not aim for crumbs; aim high, and if you are who you are meant to be, you shall conquer the world.*"

I said yes there and then to building this united world, which became my guiding principle. But I was still trying to figure out what I should do.

A Vision "What do you see?"

I wanted to become a priest.

Since I was very involved in the church, I thought my way to becoming a Changemaker was to be a Catholic priest. But my father, who noticed my talent in design, figured I might as well study it since almost every poster in the church was designed by me. In the early 2000s, the field of design education was growing in Singapore. So, I applied and was accepted.

You must know how big-headed I was by then since I was supposedly coming into a field I thought I knew very well. One of the first lessons was taught by Mr. Loh Khee Yew, an award-winning national artist and a pioneer of design education in Singapore. I consider him my Yoda for design.

Mr. Loh had asked us to design and present a poster. "This would be easy," I thought, since I have done this repeatedly. After my presentation, he looked at me and asked: "What do you see?"

His question took me aback because I expected a quick comment. Feeling somewhat irritated, I responded half-heartedly, implying it should be obvious.

Then he asked, "What did you want people to see?" I told him that I wanted people to sense the excitement.

In a Yoda-like manner, he replied: "Your sequence is wrong. If you want people to see what you see, you have to decide what matters most, then graphically determine where they will look before they can sense it."

This lesson changed my view entirely about design. Until Mr. Loh's fateful lesson, I did not realize the power of design in shaping decision-making and what it was meant to do. I could consider my design career *before* Mr. Loh and *after* Mr. Loh.

Simply put, Mr. Loh helped me understand the power of design as a method to shape minds, thinking, and approaches to drive change. His thinking provided me with a vision. I ended up not pursuing priesthood.

When I eventually founded Consulus, a global creative change firm, I realized how much impact I could have on people's lives. We created new methodologies and research approaches entirely to empower individuals and organizations to achieve change by design.

Early in the process, I understood I could not do this alone.

Unite a Core Circle

Singapore, 2009

Facing lush greenery and bright-colored blooms in the home of Florence, one of our core leaders, in an old Anglo-Malay bungalow in Singapore, I asked the partners, "Why do we exist?" Around this time, for Consulus, we knew that we were a good solutions provider but we needed clarity about our cause. This lack of confidence in ourselves led us to be part of an Australian group from 2007 to 2008. This company believed in great design but did not use its principles to change the world. So, by the end of 2008, we decided to leave that group and venture on our own again.

By this time, it was clear to us that we were not the only good company in the field of strategy and design. So, we looked deeper into what we stood for and why we should continue. We were at a crossroads.

Upon deeper discernment, we saw that the core principles of management consulting needed an update. The existing premise is focused on maximizing profit and treating people's role as a cost item.

Since I encountered the movement of unity when I was young, I have been aware of the Economy of Communion (EoC), an idea launched by Chiara Lubich in 1991, which is an economic theory based on love of neighbor and reciprocity.

Trust, good institutions, and scalable solutions for good are necessary to generate an economy for the common good. However, looking deeper into the current economic system, it made us realize that there is a greater poverty than material poverty, and that is the poverty of trust, the poverty of institutions, and the poverty of solutions.

There and then, we realized that our mission is to bring change in the consulting world because global consultants have the power to influence policymakers and leaders in shaping decisions. I understood that unless we can enter boardrooms to help them make intentional decisions for good, all admirable advocacy will be brushed aside. This is also important because some of the largest consulting firms in the world are not designed for intentional good. Some have even been implicated in cases of manipulating public policy on a wide range of issues such as corruption, migrant exploitation, and drug abuse.

Consulus aims to be the global alternative to such firms and influence the world for good.

This was not an easy decision for some partners. One left because he was keen on growth and he did not see why we needed to have such a cause to change the world. However, my two other partners, Jeffrey from Hong Kong, who led finance, and Rawi, who spearheaded operations, stayed with me because they share this vision. Both are much older than me and have very different personalities and backgrounds. We also come from diverse faiths; I am a Catholic, Jeffrey is a Methodist, and Rawi is a Muslim. However, we forged a strong bond because we believed in the vision, and I benefited from their wisdom. Together, we survived storms, but soon a bigger storm loomed that nearly killed us.

Die then Pivot

Abuja, 2024

In the outskirts of Abuja, I was seated between my European partner, Stanislav Lencz, also known as Stano, and my other partner in Africa, Dr. Andrew Kwasari, President of Sa'I Anwara 'I' Jumai Consultaire Limited (SCL).

At SCL, Andrew and his team lead a significant movement of agro-entrepreneurs in adopting regenerative agricultural practices to renew the lands in Nigeria and empower small farmers.

Stano and I had come here to launch Consulus in Nigeria and partner with SCL to bring sustainable agri-methods to the world. As part of the visit, Andrew arranged for local village leaders to meet us since their villages are involved in projects with SCL. The village leaders began the meeting with Islamic prayers followed by Christian prayers.

At that moment, my mind floated back to 2014, when I was seated in church blaming God because we were facing an unexplainable crisis. Somehow, whatever my team and I did that year, no new revenue was coming into the company. People started to leave and as the last staff member went out the door, it felt like my partners and I were on our own.

We had built an incredible culture and a great team but why were we in this conundrum? I questioned God about why he was allowing this crisis to happen to us. At that time, all I heard was a deafening silence. God did not respond to me.

During that time, due to my involvement in interreligious dialogue, I was invited to go to Rome to share my experience at a conference. But I told the organizers I had no money and my company was going through a crisis. The organizers replied that it was vital that I go and they would find some providence or funds for me. And they did. Through some fortunate series of events, I soon found myself among a small group in Domus Sanctae Marthae meeting Pope Francis, a changemaking pope elected to reform the church after a series of severe scandals. I was nervous about what I should say, so I decided to speak briefly but with passion about what I believed in and how I tried to live out my calling to bring about change through my business.

Time moved slowly and as the clock ticked, it seemed like the Pope was not coming. Then suddenly, cameramen were getting into positions. Pope Francis had arrived and even joked that he was late due to a dentist appointment. Pope Francis was patient in greeting each one of us with his bright smile. Since he did not speak English, a priest I knew translated for me. I shared what I intended to say and asked, "Holy Father, may I hug you?" He said yes, and we hugged. In that moment, I felt in my heart that all would be well.

When I came back to Singapore, that feeling never left me. I realized that I had to trust, let everything go, and start again.

I had to accept the failure of our old approach and understand that we needed to be open to new business models and ways to foster change. Providentially at this time, an overseas company asked to adopt the methods of change we developed, which paved the way for Consulus to become a network model where companies could join too—one that is not done by our own efforts but in unity with partners worldwide.

This was something I did not imagine possible.

Before 2014, Consulus' work of change was only in Southeast and South Asia. But after that year, we expanded rapidly to the rest of the world, opening up in Latin America, Europe, and the United States.

As my mind floated back to the present in Abuja, looking at Andrew on my right and Stano on my left, I understood deep in my heart what a gift that crisis was. Without losing

I would not have progressed further. We were prepared to lose everything to start again but we only succeeded in doing so because we kept to our cause, and that is to build a global movement of changing the economy for the common *good*. In return, this led us to meet a global family of Changemakers.

PART ONE: SEEING

'Gani ya kori ji'.
'Seeing beats hearing'

Hausa language, a Nigerian proverb

A Lion's Gaze

A Lion's Gaze

The rich savannah is teeming with life with sounds of birds taking flight.

A mother giraffe moves in the distance with her calf, and a watering hole is nearby. Today seems like another day.

As far as the eye can see, the beauty of the savannah unfolds.

Suddenly, sounds of furious galloping are heard.

All eyes turn toward the growing trail of a cloud of dust.

Seeing this growing cloud of dust, some of the animals started to follow in its path.

With a glorious mane, a lion's head turns towards the commotion.

He gazes into the distance with an eye to other movements trying to decipher what is going on, if it is one animal or a flock.

Soon, he sees the galloping feet of a single antelope running at top speed.

The lion licks his lips but holds his position.

As far as the lion can see, he cannot figure out who was chasing the antelope as it might not be a predator he would like to face.

The sounds of the galloping come closer; with every pound of its hooves, you can almost feel the pounding of its heart.

And for a moment, the lion seems bewildered by what he is about to witness.

From the antelope's point of view, a massive tree stands in its path, its gnarled roots reaching out like ghostly fingers. But unlike before, it felt confident in its stride and ability to avoid it.

With a primal survival instinct, the antelope pushes its body to the limit to keep pace, believing it can try to avert the immovable obstacle.

Its eyes widen in fear as it realizes it is running out of options.

With a loud thud, the antelope collided with the tree with a sickening thud. Its body crumples against the weathered bark and slumps into a lump not far from the lion.

The savannah fell silent momentarily, save for the antelope's labored breaths.

Upon seeing his unlikely good fortune, the lion lets out a roar.

The Essence of a Lion's Gaze

"I have a big question. Which is: Who runs the world?"
- Ian Bremmer, political scientist, TED2023

Like Ian Bremmer, Leonardo da Vinci had big questions about the world. The Renaissance master spent a lot of time observing the world and not limiting himself to what was defined as the arts or craftsmanship of his time. Leonardo took in everything like how nature, humans, machines, and the powers of the day behaved. Everything fascinated him.

To him, the world is filled with "creative truffles" waiting to be picked. These truffles shaped his work. He also kept illuminating insights in his notebooks that added up to thousands of written notes and sketches, the most voluminous literacy legacy of a creative mind.

Part One is about seeing the world as it is and then finding "creative truffles" to change it for good. Seeing is the first step of discerning—to see if it is a cause that you are uniquely called to pursue as a Changemaker. That is what we will explore in Part Two, which will be about finding our cause.

For now, let us widen our gaze.

See Thyself

Lions have excellent vision. With a field vision of 290 degrees, their eyes are geared for hunting with a high concentration of rod cells in their retinas, which aid in low light vision. Lions also have great awareness of their kill rate. Compared to other predators like cheetahs whose kill rate is 58%, a lion's average kill rate is only 25%. This could explain why, even with a galloping prey in its direction, the lion first observes carefully before making a move.

In short, the lion practices "know thyself," an ancient aphorism attributed to Socrates, the Greek Philosopher. It is the idea of self-awareness and knowing one's nature, character, and motivations. I might add that a person should also be keenly aware of unhealthy impulses that cause them to act without a deeper examination of their values, feelings, strengths, and weaknesses.

You must be wondering why a book that advocates for changemaking calls for non-action as the first step.

Like the lion's kill rate, too few movements succeed. The reason for this is the tendency to act without observing the deeper challenges. So, at times, what we deem as change might not have a systemic effect.

It is critical to first find what I call PersonalCORE. Here are three things you need to be able to see thyself:

Personal Ability:
- **What are your capabilities in terms of hard and soft skills?**
- **How have you been able to impact others positively based on your skills?**

Personal Influence:
- **What are the personal values and beliefs that matter to you?**
- **What communities or networks do you influence based on your beliefs and values?**

Personal Difference:
- **What is your unique role as a team player?**
- **What difference are you making in the lives of friends, communities, or organizations?**

Don't worry about not being able to answer everything. The point is to start having this deeper awareness of yourself and the situation around you.

When I was starting out, a wise entrepreneur once told me, "Lawrence, if you are desperate, don't make a move." His advice helped me immensely, so I used this set of questions to situate myself before making big decisions.

Seeing Through the Cloud of Dust

During the Cold War, the Soviet Union struggled to get ahead of the United States in terms of arms capability. But it knew the American public was paranoid about the Soviets' strengths. So, it fed into the stereotypes and had its agents create fake news about the prowess of the Soviet arsenal and mailed it to journalists in the US disguised as leaks from official sources.

The misinformation tactics were so successful in the 50s and 60s that Americans bought into how superior the Soviet Union was. But it all turned out to be a Wizard of Oz narrative where, like in the famous fairy tale, a mysterious and powerful figure runs the fictional Emerald City. The character was portrayed as fearsome but was, in truth, only an ordinary man from Omaha, Nebraska. He was feared because he used smoke and mirrors to maintain his illusion of power.

In our era of technological advancement, the tools of misinformation have become more potent. Generative AI, for instance, can be harnessed to discredit individuals on a massive scale. However, the root of the problem lies deeper in the form of persistent stereotypes that society craves to validate.

These ingrained beliefs and assumptions about certain groups of people are rooted in any society's culture, history, and social structures. These stereotypes, often unconscious or subconscious, are potent forces like loose sand that only require one violent stir. Then, they appear like a storm that can overshadow everything.

These stereotypes persist even when evidence or experience contradicts them. Many of the reasons why we cannot achieve lasting peace and economic parity stem from such deep-seated stereotypes.

Another form of a 'cloud of dust' is the phenomenon of 'solutions trending'. These are quick-fix solutions that gain popularity without thorough consideration of their long-term implications. They often promise to address systemic challenges but fail to deliver sustainable results.

This can be a populist policy where politicians promise to spend and spend without the ability to pay for them. Or outlandish entrepreneurial claims such as that of WeWork that had little difference from existing co-working space models but claimed to be game changers. WeWork raised US$ 22 billion and was backed by some of the largest investors in the world, such as Softbank. But in 2023, WeWork was declared bankrupt.

People who like to create dust always boast about speed and certainty. But everyone has limits and are not exempt from the realities of mortality, even if they seem to be the greatest empire or company in the world.

As Changemakers, we need to be able to see quickly through a cloud of dust by taking time to observe how the dust settles before making our next move.

The Art of Deciphering

Amidst the sound of clashing waters, the buzz of tourists blocking the way while adjusting their large Nikon cameras, and the stench from the river—and this is what you cannot tell from photos—Venice is indeed a labyrinth for the senses. After passing through squares and crossing bridges of all kinds, one finally arrives at almost like a shrine for Leonardo da Vinci.

Italy has a gazillion basilicas, cathedrals, and tiny niches dedicated to Jesus, Mary, and many other saints. But for a shrine of a renowned Renaissance man that is associated with Venice, this is considered a humble niche.

The shrine is like a museum of sorts dedicated to a man of extraordinary talent. So, when my then-girlfriend and now-wife suggested that we check it out, I gladly agreed because like another curious pilgrim, I felt I had come to pay my respects.

As a designer, you cannot find a closer spiritual father of the practice than Leonardo da Vinci, the Renaissance man.

You can tell from his many experiments that he was not easily satisfied with simplistic answers or assumptions.

He critically tried to observe and understand the world around him, and often questioned the norms of his time. He sought to marry art and science in his wide-ranging works from art to inventing new instruments. He saw that art could be a way to educate people about science.

The masterpiece, "The Last Supper," was a great example of this which demonstrated his scientific knowledge of perspective and scale. Leonardo's works created a new genre called the "science of painting." His scorn for theoretical book knowledge drove his cause since he preferred irrefutable facts gained from experience—and this later became known as "saper vedere," which means "having the art to see."

And isn't 'seeing' what we need today?

We have an overload of information but we can certainly do better at seeing the challenges in a deeper way and finding creative ways to solve them.

Leonardo da Vinci's time was turbulent like any other. There were numerous wars as various cities competed to be centers of power. These warring Lords often enlisted Leonardo's multidisciplinary skills and his creative approach helped his generation understand the world around them.

To decipher what is going on in the world, you need dedication. To draw realistically, Leonardo observed closely how muscles and veins moved when one clenched a fist.

He studied shadows, weights, and proportions so that his paintings became so immersive that one could get lost staring into the eyes of the Mona Lisa.

How would you know if a cause is meant for you to pursue? Ask yourself, how much do you really care about it? Soon, you will realize your depth of care is more excessive than others. To others, they may see a teeming savannah where nothing is wrong, but to you, there might be a looming threat that only your eyes can see.

Likewise, many artists in Leonardo's time did not necessarily mind that the shadows or proportions were distorted because they were simply painting based on the trends of the day. But he saw deeply and truly.

If you care enough about any issue, you will see the deeper systemic issues that others can not. You will naturally gain unique insights to decipher problems and the knowledge to act on them.

THREAD 6

Who is Behind the Antelope?

"It is our time to party big."

To the tune of *hey oh, hey oh*, the camera closes in on the top deck of a large luxury yacht stacked at sea with beautiful people dancing. This extravagant scene is from the film The Wolf of Wall Street. It shows the character Jordan Belfort, played by Leonardo di Caprio, and his character's colleague Donnie Azoff, played by Jonah Hill, celebrating their success by partying in excess and with hedonism.

The film, based on the true story of Jordan Belfort, a con artist who became famous for his fraudulent actions, was directed by acclaimed director Martin Scorsese. It cost an estimated US$ 100 million and was released in 2013 to wide acclaim.

In 2016, the Wall Street Journal published an exposé linking the person who financed the movie to the largest corruption case that implicated the Malaysian government. The financier's name is Jho Low, who had become famous in recent years due to his fondness for partying big. He, too, had a yacht named Equanimity.

People have been wondering where Low got the kind of wealth that allowed him to party with celebrities. He even offered a well-known model an 11.72-carat heart-shaped diamond worth $1.29 million engraved with her initials.

The excessive display of wealth of a mysterious man soon attracted unwanted attention. After the WSJ exposé, there was a US-led investigation into the Malaysian government's investment fund, 1Malaysia Development Berhad (1MDB), which was under the direct purview of the Prime Minister of Malaysia, Najib Razak.

In 2018, when Razak lost the general election and the premiership, the new government launched an investigation into 1MDB. Low went into hiding when an arrest warrant was issued for him. After a series of investigations, it was alleged that the Prime Minister of Malaysia and his wife were directing Low in his various activities around the world to enrich themselves. The final bill to the people of Malaysia allegedly amounted to US$ 4.5 billion stolen through 1MDB.

Full disclosure: My father was a migrant from Malaysia before becoming a Singaporean. I still have many relatives there, so this rage felt close to home.

Another example of who is behind the antelope would be the rise of OpenAI, the world's foremost brand for generative AI. When the board of OpenAI ousted its CEO, Sam Altman, it became clearer who the real power behind OpenAI was. Microsoft, who was not consulted on the board's decision, immediately provided Sam with a safe harbor and guaranteed work for anyone wishing to leave OpenAI. The board capitulated and reinstated Sam in just three days, and then the board resigned. What a powerful move by the CEO of Microsoft, Satya Nadella!

What is illuminating in these examples is that behind any obvious and galloping antelope lies a hidden power. Those hidden powers may only want to be found if necessary. So, when we observe any situation, be careful of the obvious; they are literally only the tip of the iceberg.

The Limits of Galloping

On 17 September 2011, crowds started gathering at Zuccotti Park, just a few blocks from Wall Street. This became known as Occupy Wall Street where thousands of people gathered to protest economic inequality, corporate influence in politics, and injustices in the financial system. The movement called for action against the 1% and said that this was time for the 99% to close the gap between the ultra-rich and the man on the street.

When the protests started, the media scrutiny on Wall Street was indeed high and intense. This spawned similar actions in other cities in the United States and worldwide. The momentum continued to drive the movement. As it was organized in a decentralized way, Occupy Wall Street did not manage to come to terms with the set of changes it demanded from the system it was against. Having said this, the movement, however, raised awareness of the extreme inequality of capitalism and that there was a pressing need for change.

Several months later, since the movement was leaderless, platformless, and lacking the specific policy goals that it sought to change, it started to lose momentum. On 15 November 2011, the police removed the remaining protestors from the park.

Public protests and revolutions are essential but hard to sustain to enable lasting change. Movements like *Occupy Wall Street* to *Fridays for Future* have all been led by amazing people, with the latter being prominently headed by Greta Thunberg, the young green activist who shot to fame by inspiring students to protest on Fridays to push their governments for climate action. The challenge, though, is that once media attention dies down, it is hard to sustain such public movements.

For lasting change to take root, we need to be prepared with a longer-term plan that goes into a deeper transformation of the system and be able to influence or shape decision-makers over the long term.

This is what we mean by respecting the problem. Emotions can only get you so far in mobilizing action; the key is to engineer lasting change. Fridays for Future is a good example of seeking to engineer lasting change, as it is now pivoting as a movement and becoming more thoughtful in shaping change versus the once-in-a-generation Occupy Wall Street movement.

In business, lasting change can be seen in how companies such as Alibaba and Amazon raised the livelihoods of millions of small enterprises. They created the e-commerce business entirely in a new way by rethinking processes and the ecosystem of suppliers and building the technology to sustain it.

Through my work, I have seen that while the goals of many change movements are important and necessary, too few have a systematic way of trying to succeed in the long term. This is where the gap is.

The key is ensuring that Changemakers are thinking systematically to drive change, whether it is an enterprise, non-profit work, or government service. In Consulus we use what we term as a 'serum of truth' method to judge if a change strategy is holistic; we call this the 6Ps:

Plan: Is there a clear goal and framework?

Persons: Are there people empowered to act on this?

Process: Have they thought through the process of making it work?

Practices: How are they prepared to change habits and behaviors?

Promotion: How do they intend to communicate and promote this change?

Performance: How do they measure impact?

An Overconfident Antelope

"I was also troubled by the apparent over-confidence of a generation that has only known stability, growth and prosperity. I thought our people should understand how vulnerable Singapore was and is, the dangers t hat beset us, and how we nearly did not make it."

- Lee Kuan Yew,
First Prime Minister of Singapore.

Lee Kuan Yew was so worried about the overconfidence of Singaporeans that he wrote a book titled "Hard Truths To Keep Singapore Going" after he retired as Prime Minister. He saw how overconfidence destroyed the fortunes of nations much larger than Singapore. Lee Kuan Yew and his team were constantly paranoid about Singapore's survival which was the polar opposite of overconfidence.

Lee, however, had every reason to be concerned because he and his compatriots built a city-state with few prospects after leaving Malaysia to emerge as the pre-eminent economic center of Southeast Asia. Singapore's per capita GDP jumped from around US$ 500 in 1965 to around US$ 11,800, or a staggering 2200% increase by the time Lee stepped down as PM in 1990.

Lee is an astute observer and a student of history; and history is littered with the perils of overconfidence. China's long civilizational history is a good example as a country that was better organized as a society and ahead of the West. For instance, by the early 15th century, the Ming Dynasty had 3,500 naval vessels and dominated East and Southeast Asia. But just after a century, due to corruption, palace politics, and overconfidence, it paid no attention to its fleet. Hence, it dwindled to a shadow of its former self, that even Japanese pirates easily threatened the empire.

With a weakened navy and a northern front, the Ming Dynasty gave way to the reign of the Manchus, who proclaimed themselves the Qing Dynasty. History would later repeat itself that by the early 20th century, the larger Qing Dynasty was trumped by the Japanese.

Prior to its defeat, the Beiyang Fleet, one of the four modernized fleets of the Chinese empire, was said to be the most robust naval fleet in East Asia. What was the difference then? The difference is that while Imperial China had the training and the resources, Imperial Japan's reforms went much further in terms of systemic change. In terms of the military, the latter had reorganized its entire organization of military units according to other modern armies of its time. In contrast, Imperial China's military organization was a series of sad compromises favoring tradition and its army had leaders who were not equipped to handle troops that received modern military warfare training. Pride in tradition led to the defeat of China.

It is astonishing how often great companies can forget the same strengths that brought them there.

Boeing, the pre-eminent company that built planes during the Second World War and sustained the aviation leadership of America into the 20th century, found itself in an embarrassing position in 2024 by not knowing what happened when the door of a Boeing 737 aircraft had fallen out mid-flight. The company admitted that it did not see how the plane had been put together in the first place, which astonished regulators. This rot, at the very heart of Boeing's problem, began decades ago due to overconfidence.

In pursuit of profits to shareholders and the delusional belief in its powerful brand name, Boeing decided that it could afford to reduce cost and responsibility by offshoring production capabilities to others. After it sold the facility that famously put together the nation's Boeing B-29 to a private equity firm in 2005, it completed its exit from being able to manufacture planes towards simply putting them together.

From historic missteps to present-day situations, you can be sure that overconfidence is indeed the father of all failures. Leaders do so because they sincerely believe that they will not fail or simply because they feel they will prevail and get away with it.

Bewildered? Don't be.

Growing up in the 80s, there was so much promise for the 21st century. This was supposed to be the space age. By now, we ought to have farms in orbit if you believed in the futuristic vision often depicted in the 1980s.

But, when we arrived in the 21st century, it was stunning to learn that NASA forgot how to land a human being on the moon.

Candidates for the US presidency, instead of using soaring rhetoric to conquer space, would try to out-insult one another like they were in high school.

Then you have oil companies who are leading climate change conferences, claiming to see a carbon-free future.

Today, more than a third of the world has no access to clean water and the internet.

We started with so much promise but look at where we are right now, no wonder people watch so much comedy to get through.

"Comedy doesn't change the world, but it's a bellwether."

Jon Steward, the comedian who is a giant in political satire through The Daily Show said this when he accepted the 2022 Mark Twain Award.

And rightfully so.

Because of widespread bad leadership and mediocrity, comedy became a good business, especially the kind that satirized political realities. If you take that lens to other sectors, you continue to find many comedic moments.

Human beings are a paradox; they are the only species capable of shaping complex rules and institutions for coexistence while at the same time, inventing and investing in devastating weapons systems that can, if ever deployed, annihilate the human race in minutes.

We have about 12,000 nuclear warheads held by various powers hanging over our heads. Any nuclear war, which is a frightening prospect, will be our last. Collectively, we continue to outspend on trying to kill each other rather than ending world hunger or providing clean water to those in need.

We have sufficient data on the climate crisis to know what is at stake. This is indisputable. However, all ideas are mere positions held by different people, so shouting "Shame on you!" at leaders can only go so far.

Furthermore, arguing on social media is no use in driving change in any way.

One thing is encouraging, though: if the best human minds can split the atom, there is hope that if we bring the best minds together as Changemakers, we can certainly solve the most critical challenges of poverty and the planet.

In any case, not being surprised that I can be bewildered has helped me a lot in the work of change and that is due to very human and often selfish reasons. People can do very silly things.

On the road in Abuja, Dr. Andrew Kwasari asked me to observe how some people drove in the opposite direction, endangering the lives of people, simply because they felt they had the power to. I was aware of his pain but I was not bewildered. I have seen too many people go in the opposite direction of growth.

In 2022, words like 'surprise' or 'surreal' were used when Russia invaded Ukraine, and indeed, many people, even experts, were caught off guard. It is what you would call a 'Black Swan' event.

According to Investopedia, a black swan event is defined as "extreme rarity, severe impact, and the widespread insistence they were obvious in hindsight."

What is happening to Ukraine is extremely unfortunate and yet probable. Even though we were hoping that it would not happen, it did.

So, by expecting to be bewildered from day one and knowing that people are capable of doing absolutely crazy things, we can keep up with the craziness by being intentional and serious about change.

THREAD 10

Seeing the Tree with Ghostly Fingers

There were no dry eyes among the 180 of us in the hall after a victim of the atomic bomb known as hibakusha, shared her experience of seeing fire and skin falling off of people's bodies, but more painfully, losing her family and friends. The dead filled the city's streets and canals, yet there were few people to clear them. According to her, for a long time, the city smelled of death.

Those who were killed, vaporized instantly but left ghostly shadows behind. The others who survived had to deal with the aftermath of the nuclear fallout for decades, including health problems both physical and mental.

Yet, through this end-of-times scenario, she found the extraordinary will to live on and work as an activist for peace.

Together with youth leaders from 100 countries, we gathered for the Religions for Peace World Assembly in Hiroshima and listened intently to the hibakusha's story. I internalized what I heard with great pain but also understood that this incident would not teach the world. We are still saddled with an even larger payload of nuclear warheads that can result in thousands more Hiroshimas around the globe.

The industry for arms and nuclear warheads remains formidable with the shadow of its ghostly fingers being able to reach everywhere.

In every sector and nation, the image of the tree with ghostly fingers as mentioned in the parable exists, whether it is the deep scourge of corruption or monopolies that deny smaller firms access. They are dead yet deeply rooted, and looms large over many systems.

You may hear calls for change occasionally, but like nuclear disarmament, it is easier to pay lip service than having to actually do it.

In our two decades of work, I have observed that there are three types of change:

Touch-up Change: This means that resistance is highest even at the leadership levels. In this case, any call for change is primarily a communications exercise but parallel power structures remain. Change in real terms is only up to 5% of the environment or organization only.

Transformational Change: This means that in certain areas where the leadership tolerates change, as long as it does not touch the sensitive parallel structures, it can go ahead. This could be done by changing only a strategic area, so change in real terms is only up to 30% of the environment or organization.

Transfigurative Change: This means that leadership at the highest level is vulnerable to admitting that deep systemic issues exist and need to be resolved. From leadership to principles of change, the core team is committed and united in delivering outcomes, shaping behaviors, and redesigning system processes. This ensures the rise of an internal movement, and change, in real terms, can be up to 60-70% of the environment or organization.

Sadly, we have far too many claims of change that are in the Touch-up state and too few in the Transfigurative state.

With even fewer Changemakers who are willing to beat the odds, we need to have the vision and posture of a lion. Because of the limited number of Changemakers, we must be deliberate in our intentions and clearly observe where to aim for key wins.

What Dead Antelopes Can Teach You

The air was still and I was going nowhere with the session until I asked the participants about their kids instead of talking more about the bank. The conversations soon became chirpy as the mothers in the group spoke over one another, sharing their hearts about their children and their hopes for them.

I felt I had unlocked something new, even though this should have been obvious as Brunei is very family-oriented. Until then, our long-drawn research of almost eight months got us nowhere on how to ignite a change movement in the bank.

This humbling experience was part of our transformation project for a Southeast Asian bank that sought to reshape its digital, brand, and customer engagement strategy through a systematic design-thinking method, also known as 'business design.'

We then changed the core driving strategy for the bank to *doing it with your heart to inspire the next generation*. The shift in approach helped unite the different factions during the change process because it was no longer about a better bank, but a bank for their families and something they could relate to. Now, the bank is an award-winning institution with an extensive social impact program. This experience affirmed my belief of the importance of accepting failures early and making a shift towards a better direction. Or what I might describe as recognizing the 'dead antelopes' and doing something different.

There is indeed a lot to learn from dead antelopes, as in past failures. By being a good student of why certain things fail, it can help to illuminate our present day solutions. But too many prefer to talk about successes and avoid talking about failures, because like a dead antelope, they smell.

In 2019, the Chairperson of the World Economic Forum, Klaus Schwab said that the global system has spun out of control and shared his ideas on how we can balance it. He listed the usual headline global challenges faced by society such as technology, inclusion, climate change, and economic growth. More importantly, he called for new ways to solve our common problems. He cited that we need to respect diversity when we collaborate, to involve people at all levels of society, and to be inclusive, gender-balanced, ethical, and human-centered.

Schwab's call highlighted an admission that the usual economic instruments of free trade, shared global standards, and the information highway have not made much headway in terms of inclusion. In a disruptive age, this calls for a new approach to the issues of our time.

In a way, Schwab acknowledged the many dead antelopes in the room.

Let's draw inspiration from present-day examples of learning faster from failures. Consider SpaceX and Blue Origin. Both companies share similar purposes. Blue Origin, with its early start and abundant resources, spent more time sharing ideas and concepts for landing on the moon. In contrast, SpaceX embraced a different approach. It spent more time learning from failures, exploding things, and using that experience to guide itself closer and closer to its cause of conquering space. This example underscores the importance of learning from failures and should motivate us to adopt a similar mindset in our own endeavors.

Too many Changemakers try to bring about change by doing the same thing repeatedly. We cannot truly bring about the success we wish to see without recognizing where we might have failed.

Widening Your Gaze Strategically

Whenever I conduct a strategy workshop for clients, my team and I always prepare a section of considerations known as the Operating Dimension (OP). The OP examines the probable trends and changing realities such as:

Political: Examine how political issues can impact what you do

Technology: Analyze how technology will shape behaviors and needs

Social: Assess how societal trends will shape identity and relationships

Competition: Understand how competition has changed

These four aspects explore whether the current OP will likely be advantageous to the change model or highly detrimental to its existence. The OP has been used in our 20 years of work in advising governments, businesses, and non-profits globally. We keep updating our view of the world to note changing realities.

Over the years, after presenting the OP, I have observed that people often exhibit the following three kinds of mindsets:

1. The Supremo Mindset: Highly dismissive as they assume they will reign supreme in all scenarios

This group is confident that their operating model will always be relevant and that nothing can ever cut it down to size. Their response to the OP is always, "I have seen this, and my experience tells me the trends you mention here will never happen!" They tend to not give room for discussion as they must always have the last word.

2. The Defeatist Mindset: Fully cognizant but has a negative mentality

This group will fully understand and agree with the OP presented. But they go to the extreme and assume that reality cannot be shaped or changed and that they are doomed. They will not entertain further discussion because they have written themselves off.

3. The Strategic Mindset: Full awareness and strategic thinking

Then there are the few who thoroughly know their vulnerabilities and strengths. They are determined to face the realities to overcome them by refusing to accept the current condition or trends as inevitable.

In terms of nation-building, an example would be Singapore, where Prime Minister Lee Kuan Yew and his colleagues, such as Goh Keng Swee, thought of creative ways to help Singapore survive and thrive. They saw that it was possible to convert smallness into an advantage by proving to be agile and innovative to fit the needs of global investors. Their strategies proved that size does not matter; mindset does. As a result, Singapore continues to punch above its weight today because of its strategic moves.

Whatever life may throw at you, remember that nothing is ever a done deal. What matters is your mindset. Be strategic, not a defeatist; do not be a supremo. Being strategic means never assuming since everything is possible. In life, we will face a few black swans. It is best to meet them strategically.

Changemaking with a Lion's Gaze

In the journey of changemaking, let us reflect on the nine ways to widen our gaze, starting from ourselves and opening our worldview.

Personal Gaze

i.   Begin by seeing thyself.

ii. Where are the clouds of dust fogging your view?

iii. Assess your genuine interest in the art of seeing.

Situational Gaze

iv. Are you able to see who is behind the antelope?

v.   Do you see where the short-term galloping is?

vi. Do you see overconfidence and its effects?

Systematic Gaze

vii. Where are the trees with ghostly fingers?

viii.What can dead antelopes teach you?

ix. Widen your gaze strategically.

It is through seeing with a discerning gaze that we can discover our cause, which is the next step.

PART TWO: CAUSE

"जीवन भनेको पहाड चढ्नु जस्तै हो, शिखरमा पुग्नको लागि
दृढ संकल्प र स्पष्ट दृष्टि चाहिन्छ।"
(Nepali proverb)

"Life is like climbing a mountain,
you need determination and a clear
vision to reach the top."

Tenzing Norgay

Find Your Everest

Find Your Everest

The air is thin, and here, the peaks kiss the heavens. It is a sight to behold.

Amidst this heavenly sight, though, Nat, who is heaving and struggling, has no time to take stock.

She will be content if she can reach for just one more step before a critical rest.

"Need a hand, friend?" Pasang, Nat's sherpa, asked with a knowing smile.

The Sherpas are people who have lived in the Himalayas for centuries, so this is their backyard.

Nat took it and together, they arrived at South Col, about 26,000 feet above sea level.

This is a place to rest and prepare for the ultimate challenge: the death zone.

A zone with a severe drop in oxygen that can lead to altitude sickness, frostbite, and other life-threatening conditions.

Not to mention unpredictable conditions such as sudden storms and high winds.

Nat knows the risk very well; she attempted Everest twice before but gave up before even arriving at the death zone.

This is the highest she has ever been, thanks to Pasang.

But for now, rest is in order.

After setting up their tents and securing them well with Guy Lines, Nat finally settled for a meal.

Turning to Pasang, she asked, "How do you people do this? This is like a walk in the park for you."

Pasang replied, "Our people are born here; we are the daughters and sons of these sacred peaks. We were meant for these paths; we need less oxygen because it is in our DNA. But what about you? Why is a girl from London doing this?"

Nat paused and said, "My father climbed Everest, and from a young age, I felt called to do the same. But I am not like my father; he is a hero, and I am much lesser. "

"You should not compare yourself with him; one of the essences of climbing Mount Everest is not to conquer it but to let it become one with your being," Pasang replied.

"If you have prepared physically well, the next thing is to prepare your heart and mind. Is this your cause? If this cause belongs to someone else, it is better not to proceed. Everyone I accompanied to climb these paths has found their reason to go on to the next. The final zone will be much more about the heart and mind."

Nat thanked Pasang for the encouragement.

The next day, as light dawned, Mount Everest seemed to beckon with fine weather.

Nat and Pasang began their ascent through the death zone.

But the sacred Everest was relentless; obstacles after obstacles remained in their path. Avalanches threatened to bury them, crevasses yawned hungrily beneath their feet, and fierce winds howled like vengeful spirits.

Yet through it all, Nat remembered Pasang's words: find your own path and remain steadfast.

Pasang's astute sense of where to reach or step certainly helped.

After what felt like an eternity, they reached the summit, the pinnacle of their journey stretching out in a breathtaking panorama of snow-capped peaks and endless sky.

Nat collapsed to her knees, tears of joy and relief streaming down her face as she took in the magnitude of the moment.

She had become one with her Everest.

The Essence of Cause

"Only one who devotes himself to a cause with his whole strength and soul can be a true master. For this reason, mastery demands all of a person."

- Albert Einstein, theoretical physicist

After having advocated and led the systematic implementation of purpose-driven strategy for personal and corporate growth for almost 20 years, I realized that there is a difference between the concept of purpose and cause. And it is stark.

You may help a person or an organization discern a purpose, and identify with it, and that purpose provides clarity; it is the "why" orientation toward growth. However, compared to cause, it has a lower effect on mobilizing change and action.

Any cause, if it is truly needed, is more demanding. It is existential, larger than one person or a group, and is almost like an atomic effect versus purpose, which tends to be more conventional. Furthermore, a clear and powerful cause can unleash incredible energy over a longer term and have broader mobilization effects.

This is the common characteristic of a Changemaker—the extraordinary ability to put their entire strength and soul into a greater cause that summons a movement more significant than themselves.

A sign that you are meant to pursue a particular cause is the ability to generate a creative vision. We will explore that later in Part Three, but for now, let us discern our cause.

Causes are Born Out of Contests

The contest of wills between the Indian plate and the Eurasian plate, over millions of years of tectonic activity, resulted in the high mountain peaks of the Himalayas.

When I was in Kathmandu for a campaign event on Arms Down in 2010, the place where we were meeting had a window view of Mount Everest. It was a cloudy day and as the clouds slowly parted, I pointed at what looked like the summit and asked my friend if that was indeed the peak of the infamous mountain. He moved my hand higher and said, "not there, but here." The scale was so majestic that I stood in awe and as the sky cleared, I saw its immensity, and had no doubts as to why it is considered the world's rooftop.

In Nepali, the peak is also known as "Sagarmatha," which translates to "forehead of the sky," and rightfully so, given its proximity to the sky.

The mission of the Economist Magazine reads:

"a severe contest between intelligence, which presses forward, and an unworthy, timid ignorance obstructing our progress."

What a great statement that defines the cause of the Economist Magazine. It is a clear example of what a good cause worth pursuing looks like.

Like Everest, many causes throughout history were born through contests that took a long time before rising as mountains. Causes like those that fought for the end of slavery, which was a norm in the past, took centuries to actualize, and although modern slavery persists, the fight continues.

The rise of mountains also draws on powerful and fiery forces deep within the Earth. These forces can rise to the top and their fury can dramatically remake the landscape.

Since time immemorial, forces with a negative cause have used fear and hatred to assert control and dominance, while forces with a positive cause have inspired hope, love, and freedom to summon their movements for change.

Erected after the Second World War to divide between the West and the communist Soviet Union, the Berlin Wall not only stood as a security border, it was a distinct marker between hope and fear, between freedom and dictatorship.

But on 9 November 1989, in footage seen by unbelieving eyes around the world, East and West Berliners stood on the wall. On any other day, no one would even dare go near it as this would put them in a position to be killed. Instead, people were cheering and chipping away at the wall.

Amidst all this, the hope that the people in the East held on to prevailed. This hope pushed away the fear of death and urged thousands to cross the heavily guarded wall. The fall of the Berlin Wall resulted in a domino effect where many Soviet states demanded independence in search of freedom.

How do you recognize a cause? You recognize it by the gravity of the issue and whether there is an equally opposing force. If it is a worthy cause, you will find an equally powerful opposing force.

A Sherpa Whose Critique Strengthens Your Resolve

When I studied design, I learned the importance of good critique, a practice necessary to great creative work. First, we were taught how to subject ourselves to critique. Then, we learned how to execute it effectively. Many people pay a lot of attention to user-centered design, but the most useful part of my training as a professional designer was learning the critique method.

To succeed in your cause, you need a trusted person with the necessary experience to give helpful critique. It does not matter whether you take the person's advice or not. What matters is that they are offering it from a position of experience which can shape your decision making and help you in your endeavor.

This is akin to the Sherpas, who have lived in the Himalayas for hundreds of years and have deep roots in the Tibetan plateau. They have dwelled among the peaks long enough and their bodies have uniquely adapted to the region's low oxygen levels. Therefore, their expertise as guides and porters for climbers is invaluable.

Before Steve Jobs was preparing to return to Apple, he sought advice from Larry Ellison, another entrepreneur who founded a great company and made complex deals. The wonderful thing about this relationship is even though Steve was clear-eyed about his goals, he wanted feedback from someone who is experienced in such scenarios.

Larry, on the other hand, was eager to help his friend to be done with the process by simply helping him buy Apple, whose stock was going badly anyway. Steve Jobs thought about it deeply yet preferred to be invited back to Apple as he was not into hostile takeovers.

A year later, Steve Jobs was invited back to Apple.

Larry was curious and asked if neither he nor Steve owns Apple, how will they make money? Then Steve leaned in and said that if both of them did not own Apple, he would have a moral high ground. Larry was astonished and went on to remark:

"Steve, that's really expensive real estate, this moral high ground."

Steve would follow through with this pursuit of the moral high ground by taking only $1 as a salary from 1997 until his resignation in 2011. This approach endeared him to his core team at Apple and exemplified that he was indeed cause-driven.

In this case, his resolve and plan of action was helped by his conversations with Larry, who had the means and know-how to pull off a hostile takeover if he ever needed it. Though Steve did not take Larry's advice, he knew he could have but still chose to do things differently from a moral high ground.

So, finding someone whose advice comes from experience, makes a difference.

A Worthy Cause Outweighs the Risks

After carefully examining a situation and discerning your own strengths and weaknesses, you will eventually decide if the cause is worth it and outweighs the risks. This happened to me when I was a member of the Designers Association Singapore (DAS), one of the oldest creative associations of designers.

The association gave me a head start as a young designer in 2003. Everyone there was either a design entrepreneur or a design professional, and they were generous in their mentorship to help a youngling like me. I was recruited into the group simply because one of the Executive Council members, Alexander Lau, said: "You do not know what difference you can bring, and actually, you can." I replied that I was not sure but that I would try.

The association provided me with a platform and access to practitioners with market experience, which helped me immensely in my early years as a design startup. In 2009,

DAS, elected me as their president. By this time, the organization had been under crisis—membership was in free fall and the group was seen as an old boys club. This was also why I was elected. They wanted a younger person to revive the standing of a 24-year old association. However, having been in the association for a few years, I knew the deeper issue was a lack of trust and a common cause to shape the industry's future. Ultimately, DAS was not sustainable because it was not properly organized to bring in a diversity of members to take it to the next level.

I had my work cut out for me.

First, I worked hard to demonstrate to every member that we cannot look at our association with the same lens as before while also listening to their concerns. At the same time, I worked with a few core leaders, like my Vice President, Ulrich Schraudolph, a brilliant and seasoned industrial designer from Germany with years of experience in Singapore; Alexander Lau, the one who recruited me and a skilled industrial designer; and Florence Oh, a seasoned media executive. I also got my partner from Consulus, Jeffrey to support us on financial issues. Together, we slowly nursed the association back to health with a series of initiatives to promote the industry and unite the community.

Even though the association claimed to be the association for all designers, it did not include architects, as the latter had their own group. Hence, to truly unite and broaden the base to include all professional designers, we had to take more risks and change the constitution.

Several voices were against it but we lobbied hard and won the vote.

We also saw that if the association only spoke to designers without involving the wider business community, we would be irrelevant because most of the time, the conversation focused on self-preservation and not about influencing the business community.

So this time, a bolder change was proposed: renaming the association to Design Business Chamber Singapore (DBCS) and updating the constitution to allow businesses with design teams to join. This was the most controversial change I proposed where I was subjected to some personal attacks. It was even more painful because the comments came from seniors I looked up to in the industry. The most brutal pain comes from the ones you seek to love.

Yet despite everything, we emerged victorious. We won the vote.

It has been over a decade since I finished my term and handed over the chamber in good hands. Today, DBCS is Singapore's leading multidisciplinary design chamber, with a renowned standing and a network of large companies. Its annual award-giving body, SG Mark, is participated by leading companies in Singapore who demonstrate how they shape the world for good through design and creative projects.

In sum, while it is true that the cause outweighs the risks, there are decisions that only you can make.

To Others, This is a Death Zone; To You, This is Paradise

As far as the eye can see, you alone are responsible for managing the landing and taking off of multiple aircrafts carrying thousands of people. In a busy airport such as Changi or Heathrow, in addition to the high workload, changing conditions and unexpected events can affect your decisions. So, you need to be good at multitasking and making quick decisions while bearing in mind the safety of thousands of people. To many of us reading this, this is a nightmarish scenario; to a select few, though, they are able to summon their calm and go about their job just like any other day.

Similarly, there are so many jobs in the world where you cannot imagine how people do it.

How do chefs face heat in commercial kitchens that go up to 45°C while churning out dish after dish amidst the loud sounds of clanging metalware?

Then you have surgeons and nurses in emergency departments or war zones who battle against time to save lives. Yet they are calm under duress because they know that this is their cause.

The list goes on.

So, the litmus test for knowing whether a cause is meant for you to pursue on a lifelong basis or not, is whether it evokes a fight-or-flight mentality in you.

If you struggle daily to go to work or have second thoughts on what you are supposed to do, you might be involved in an aspirational cause but it may just not be meant for you.

However, if you are aware of the pain, the struggles, the disappointments that lie ahead yet still feel a special kind of joy that only you can understand, even if it sounds wild and absurd, then that is a sign that what you are doing is your vocation.

According to the Cambridge Dictionary:

Vocation is defined as a type of work that you feel you are suited to doing and to which you should give all your time and energy, or the feeling that a type of work suits you in this way.

In short, finding your vocation, being in a workplace where you feel you are home despite the odds or difficulty, is your paradise.

Recognizing your vocation matters greatly for a cause because it will be a battle of wills.

When asked what advice he would give to Stanford students, Jensen Huang, the CEO of Nvidia said, "I wish upon you ample pain and suffering."

This is so true if you look at it objectively. There is pain in everything. There is pain in the people you love, in the organizations you are involved in, and the issues you are passionate about.

In my work with organizations I care about, the greatest pain came from being maligned by the people I admire. But I intuitively understood that this was what I signed up for and that it was what I had to live with.

What about you? Where is your paradise?

The Dots From the Past Will Lead to Your Cause

"You can't connect the dots looking forward; you can only connect them looking backward. So you have to trust that the dots will somehow connect in your future. You have to trust in something — your gut, destiny, life, karma, whatever. This approach has never let me down, and it has made all the difference in my life."

- Steve Jobs,
Commencement address to Stanford students,
12 June 2005

Whether it is the evolution of our abilities, our belief systems, or the way we navigate ourselves based on the difference we seek to be, our past has led us to our present.

Steve's experience at Reed College was where he discovered the beauty of typography, which ultimately made its way into Mac computers and allowed Apple to lead the industry by being at the intersection of technology and the liberal arts.

Then it was his personal experience of being booted out of Apple that helped him find himself and enabled him to found two other companies: Pixar, one of the world's most successful animation studios, and NeXT, whose world-class technology was acquired by Apple, which led to his return to the company he founded and loved.

He kept faith in his cause, which helped him greatly in return.

In a similar way, Lee Kuan Yew's experience of the Second World War helped to 'steel' himself up and allowed him to see that the sun had indeed set on the mighty British empire.

When he subsequently studied in London, he met other young peers who were all caught up in the independence movement post-World War. So many students from around the world were studying in London then whose views and orientation would eventually impact the world. During that time, he gained the network and the confidence to engage in debates about remaking the new world that was emerging from the war.

Lee met his compatriots by joining the Malayan Forum, an anti-colonial group. This forum was founded by Goh Keng Swee, Singapore's first finance minister and economic czar, who would eventually become Lee's partner in building Singapore.

When Lee subsequently returned to Singapore and practiced law, he intuitively understood that he had to fight for the social justice of the workers.

Eventually, it became clear that if he wanted to bring about real change, he had to participate in the political process, present his case, and seek public support. This led to the founding of the People's Action Party with his friends.

The war experience, being amid the energy of independence movements, his unique network of friends, and his expertise as a competent lawyer gave him the best set of tools to pursue his cause.

"At the end of the day, what have I got? A successful Singapore. What have I given up? My life."

- Lee Kuan Yew, Founding Prime Minister of Singapore

Your Everest is Yours Alone to Pursue

In the midst of hushed voices, we were in the cafeteria of Domus Sanctae Marthae, the place where the Pope usually eats. I am here for a major meeting of the Vatican's Dicastery for Interreligious Dialogue. I was seated next to a few cardinals and religious nuns under a beautifully lit centerpiece.

Although Pope Francis was not with us for lunch, as a papal fan, I became curious to know where the Pope usually sits when he eats.

One priest, a regular at the cafeteria, gestured to a table in a dimly lit corner. 'That's where the Pope dines," he said. "Alone."

"We give him space," the priest continued, "and try not to disturb him too much. But, of course, people still go and greet him."

This simple gesture of providing him with own space made me realize the weight of his responsibilities and the isolation that comes with leadership. Pope Francis was elected at a time of crisis in the Catholic Church. His predecessor resigned and the last time a pope resigned was 600 years ago. The Church was also beset by financial and sex scandals. But there he was in the midst of it all, a Pope elected by the College of Cardinals to lead a 1.3 billion-member church, the largest and oldest institution in the world.

In a sense, his cause is that of change, albeit in a familiar territory like the Catholic Church whose founder was also seen as a Changemaker himself. Then there were the critics. Pope Francis has, from time to time, personally expressed frustration at the attacks that come at him. In a certain sense, he is alone.

Jesus said, "Whoever wishes to come after me must deny himself, take up his cross, and follow me," which is a hard act to follow if you know what the crucifixion meant. Ultimately, the decision to face the 'Everest' or challenging setbacks of your cause, is yours to make.

From time to time, I engage in conversations with the leaders I work with. Once, we were working on transforming a conservative national bank in Southeast Asia. In a one-to-one dialogue with Javed, the CEO, I assessed the odds stacked against us in shaping change for the company, such as:

- **The limiting regulatory environment**
- **A transactional culture without purpose**
- **Few prospects for additional growth**

These underlying issues, coupled with government and bureaucratic-related issues, made the task at hand even more daunting. So I asked him, given the odds, if we should aim for a minimum change in the company or opt for bigger and lasting ones. Javed calmly admitted that while the odds are real, it is essential that the change continues no matter how long, or challenging, it is. If it succeeds, then it will be an excellent example of how a slow, conservative bank can transform.

I was so inspired by his openness and honesty that we committed ourselves to working with him to realize the change he envisioned. Over five years, we overcame one challenge at a time, and today, that bank, Bank Islam Brunei Darussalam (BIBD), is a leading institution for the nation and, indeed, a perfect example of conquering Everest.

From this experience, I learned that leaders who are comfortable being alone in confronting existential truths are capable of shaping lasting, fundamental change.

Mount Everest Will Beckon with Fine Weather if Your Cause is True

In a dimly lit windowless room with an overhung lamp, I imagined myself about to go through an FBI-style interrogation. Seated across the table with a paper in hand, he looked at me coldly in the eyes and barked:

"Do you know what you have done? You have failed and your learning journey ends here! You can never get back into the system!"

My lecturer delivered this cold, hard truth Singapore-style because I failed my examinations to pursue a course in the polytechnic I did not choose—marine engineering. I was assigned to it because I did not do well in my examinations prior to entering the polytechnic.

As I left the room, I felt a cold chill down my spine. I thought my world had crashed then because in my little island of unforgiving change, failure was not an option for me.

That was in 1997.

As I sat in the brightly lit Clementine Hall in the Vatican in 2022, where Kings and Emperors met Popes and history was made, I thought of that moment in 1997.

Fortunately, my journey did not end there and then.

I found my footing again by keeping faith in my cause. I wanted to build a united world but I needed to find my place in the world first. Because of that failure, I had to enter the army early in 1997. But before going in, someone advised me that even in the army, I, too, could continue my cause of building a united world. I was surprised yet still tried.

The army experience was great. I rose up through the ranks, winning two awards for best cadet, and surprisingly, I was able to do what I love, which is design.

After serving in the armed forces, I applied to study design, but I still wanted to know how I could bring about a united world through what I did.

In that school, I met Mr. Loh Khee Yew, who powerfully changed my mind about the power of design and creativity in changing the world. Mr. Loh's thinking greatly influenced me when I eventually built my business once I realized how much impact I could have in people's lives.

I saw design not for what it could do but for what it could be to help people see the truth of their situations and guide their way forward. It became my life's work and my firm's to figure out how to help people discern their strategy for change. We created methodologies and research approaches to help organizations transform through creative change.

Singapore has since become a much more forgiving place. I have built a global business, met Changemakers, the Pope, a Sultan, Presidents, and CEOs, and worked with entire change movements in businesses, non-profits, and governments. I did not come from a background of privilege; I was born to migrant parents from Malaysia and my own experience showed me that being cause-driven and creative can give you the power to move mountains.

So don't worry. As my favorite actor, Tom Hanks, once said, "This too shall pass."

Facing Obstacles with Cause-fueled Resilience

When the COVID-19 pandemic halted the world, we were deeply involved in helping many global companies, especially vulnerable social enterprises, pivot in their businesses to keep them going through the support of governments and working with business associations.

The audit covered 12 aspects of how COVID-19 has impacted them, namely:

Employees: Assess the strength of relationships in these trying times

Suppliers: Assess the strength of relationships with suppliers to obtain mutually favorable terms

Clients: Assess the strength of relationships with customers

Partners: Assess the type of strategic partnerships that can aid the business

Financial Sustainability: Assess how long they can last in these trying times

Sales: Assess the impact on sales and activities

Operations: Assess COVID-19's effect on operations

Digitalization: Assess the company's ability to pivot with digital tools quickly

Marketing: Assess the effectiveness of marketing efforts

Quality: Assess how COVID-19 will impact the delivery of goods

Product/Service Innovation: Assess the ability to roll out new products and services within 3-6 months

Industry Pivot: Assess the ability to enter a related industry based on strengths

This audit had to be done within a week. From 2020 - 2021, we reviewed companies from the Americas, Asia, and Europe and discovered why some companies are more resilient than others.

No one expected that the pandemic would last for two years. Based on evidence and facts, we discovered that the more resilient companies possessed these four Cs:

1. They were cause-driven
2. They had a culture of trust
3. They were creative in their vision for the business
4. They were able to pivot competently

But the biggest factor of all is being cause-driven because everyone knew what they were fighting for, even during the pandemic. This singular factor helped these enterprises navigate and make better decisions amid emerging problems that came one after another due to COVID-19.

This translated well into mindsets, too; being cause-driven helped keep the teams together and strengthen their resolve, which paved the way for better communication even though people were not in the same location.

Being cause-driven helps you become resilient.

Your Cause Will Help You Remain Steadfast

"You may not arrive yet at where you wish to be
but you can be fully present; you can feel it; it is there
even as you move, when you feel the back of your sole
touch the floor till the front of your feet lands, you can
feel the present all the way to your toes. There, in this feeling,
is your divine present; it is here where you and your
moment are one"

- Buddhist Monk

This is what a Thai Buddhist monk said to me during an interreligious meeting when I asked about how he prays and stays in the present. Initially, my mind went, "wow!", since I knew that I was still incapable of this skill.

We were together in Rome in memory of Chiara Lubich, my hero who inspired me with the cause of building a united world.

She founded a movement for unity during the Second World War. Even though she is Catholic, in this movement called the Focolare, which means the "hearth or a fireplace," there were members of other religions and even those without religion.

I found resonance with what this monk shared as Chiara Lubich often talked about living in the present moment. She explained once by saying:

> *"Imagine you are on a train. Even if you walk up or down, you cannot make the train go faster, so be present and stay present. That is your moment with God."*

Chiara Lubich can certainly say a lot about the present moment because the Catholic Church that she loved so much all her life once banned her from her beloved movement. After the Second World War, even though she made a personal vow of chastity and poverty to dedicate her life to God, and she founded a community of people who started to spread the idea of building a united world, she was not in any recognized structures or religious order of the Church. A group of girls started leaving their families to follow her, yet they were not religious nuns. Because they read the bible on their own without a priest and talked about unity, the authorities in the church suspected that she was either a Protestant, Communist, or a heretic that led people astray.

After an investigation, she was told by the authorities to resign from the Focolare Movement.

She was devastated but because she was so sure of her cause and her calling, she quietly convinced herself that one day, all would be well. It was only after several years later that she was reinstated and her movement warmly embraced by the Catholic Church. She became a confidante to Popes, Orthodox, and Protestant leaders. Her movement took off to the ends of the earth.

When she died in 2008, the New York Times called her one of the most powerful women in the Roman Catholic Church.

If your cause is true, it will help you remain steadfast, and you will prevail.

Changemaking with a Cause

While everyone can discern their purpose, having a cause is something else. It is external and greater and can generate an atomic effect, but it is also demanding. So, discern carefully if this is your way by:

Recognizing your cause
i.   Mountains are born out of contests; what is the gravity of your cause?
ii. Who is the sherpa who can strengthen your resolve?
iii. With full appreciation of the risks, will you still chase your cause?

Defining your cause
iv. You will know if this is your vocation.
v.   You will gradually be able to connect the dots.
vi. Ultimately, you will come to a moment to make a choice.

Being empowered by your cause

vii. Your cause will help you be creative.

viii.Resilience is a sign of your cause.

ix. If your cause is confirmed, you will remain steadfast.

If you are who you are meant to be, you will see a creative vision that others have not. We will explore this in the next part.

"If you are working on something
exciting that you really care about,
you don't have to be pushed.
The vision pulls you."

Steve Paul Jobs,

Founder of Apple

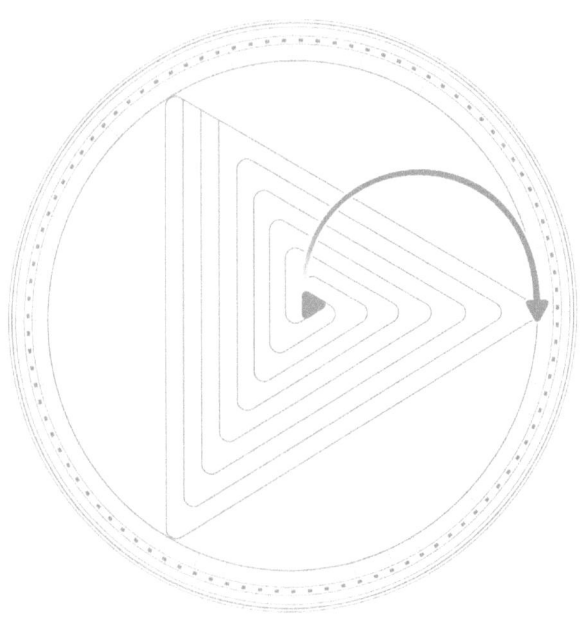

Build Your Cathedral

A Soaring Vision

Amidst echoes of hammering and chiseling, a man with fine shoes navigates the labyrinthine corridors of scaffolding and workmen. A wealthy merchant, Henri de Marchand, stops for a moment to admire the lights and shadows that come off rising stone walls, which are crafted to precision to eventually meet as arches for a grand church.

He has been traveling to different worksites to learn about the construction of Gothic cathedrals, for he dreams of building one even grander than Cathédrale Notre-Dame. But first, he is in search of a good master mason, and he hopes he might find one here.

"And how may I help you, Monsieur?" a man asked Henri.

"Good day to you, sir," Henri noticed that the man was holding the plans for the cathedral and could be the person he was looking for. "I am Henri de Marchand, a merchant of some means from the neighboring town of Tours. I seek to commission the construction of a new cathedral in Tours that will rival the grandeur of Cathédrale Notre-Dame. I have the resources to fund such a project, but what I lack is the guidance and skill of a master mason such as the one who is directing this fine worksite."

Phillipe, the master mason, replied, "It is more than money that you will need. Building a cathedral is a monumental task, requiring vision, patience, and persuasion. It is far more complex and challenging than people can fathom. This worksite, for instance, might have to halt soon due to differences among the people involved, such are the intricacies of such a project."

"Master Mason, I do know the difficulties of such an undertaking and the amount of effort needed to negotiate and bring people together for such a task. I have traversed far and wide to the East. It was my ability to gain the trust of friends and foes that allowed me to do well in my business of trading gemstones and fine clothes," Henri replied.

"I am also undertaking this project sincerely in memory of my late wife. She was a woman of great faith and devoted to the welfare of the people of Tours. Her passing left a void, but also inspired the people in Tours with her deep faith. They, too, support me in this noble endeavor."

"Well then, with the right motive and the support of the people and your skill in finding the resources, this is a viable task. A grand cathedral will take hundreds of years to complete, well beyond our years; it is only possible if we can convince everyone to stay the course," Phillipe replied.

"So when can we begin?" Henri asked.

Essence for Creative Vision

*"The architect must be a prophet... a prophet in
the true sense of the term... if he cannot see at least
ten years ahead, don't call him an architect."*

*- Frank Lloyd Wright,
American architect*

The famed architect's quote can be applied to every Change-maker who seeks to convince a core circle to abandon what they are doing and pursue a newfound cause with their lives. The burden is on the Changemaker to sketch out a vision to inspire change and action.

This is precisely the mission of a Gothic cathedral. You may not be able to see God, but stand under a ribbed vault and it will lead your vision upwards. Contemplate the colored rays coming through stained glass, and you will start to be filled with awe. Through immersive ways, you can soon feel that you have stepped into a divine presence.

Steve Jobs, a visionary leader, was known for his reality distortion expertise which led his team to create extraordinary products that were unimaginable at the time, but he saw it first in his mind. The power of a vision lies in not just seeing it, but in convincing others to see it too. Without heart, no one can sustain a commitment for over half a century or more.

The litmus test of a truly creative vision is when, even after the visionary is gone, the vision continues to be built by a dedicated circle of individuals. This 'circle of trust' is crucial in sustaining a vision, and in the next chapter, we will explore further into that concept.

But for now, let us talk about people who built soaring visions.

A Prophet with an Inspiring Vision

The word 'prophet' is generally skewed towards religious purposes. But its origins, as defined by Dictionary.com,

> *was first recorded in 1150–1200; Middle English prophete, from Late Latin prophēta, from Greek prophétés, equivalent to pro- "before (in time, place, precedence, dignity)" + -phētēs "speaker," derivative of phánai "to speak"*

A prophet focuses on foretelling and having a vision of the world to come.

Interestingly, around the same period the word was first used, Northern Europe saw the rise of new ways of building churches due to rising prosperity. There was a convergence of new technology, building techniques, and more importantly, money. In other words, the technology at that time allowed prophetic visions to be realized. Much like how we benefit from the wonders of generative AI today, which is the fruit of decades of development in artificial intelligence.

What defines Gothic architecture is the pointed or ogival arch. The use of this form allows the construction of tall towers with stained glass and subsequently created a competition of sorts among sponsoring parties on who could build taller towers of artistic splendor. This was no different from the skyscraper race in New York from the late 19th century to the early 20th century. Gothic cathedrals were the skyscrapers of Europe in the Middle Ages.

Now, why is this entirely relevant in the case of bringing about change? Forces with a negative cause will paint a world bound to fail and present a tower of doom. For Changemakers with a positive cause, we have to be able to overcome that with a soaring 'cathedral of hope.' In the Middle Ages, cathedrals brought comfort to people who did not have large, comfortable houses. As the cities were crowded, the cathedrals gave them hope and something to aspire to.

"Life can not just be about solving one miserable problem after another, that can't be the only thing," he says. "There need to be things that inspire you, that make you glad to wake up in the morning and be part of humanity."

- Elon Musk

This mindset is also what every successful Changemaker has done. Whether it is Martin Luther King or Malala Yousafzai, they are all 'prophets' who saw the possibilities and presented something inspiring and hopeful.

So, does your vision inspire hope?

A Vision From Navigating
Labyrinthine Corridors

Much has been written about Steve Job's genius, leadership, and creativity. But not much has been credited to his methodical way of seeing the present and the future. Tim Cook described Steve as having the rare skill of seeing around corners. This was something I highlighted in my first TEDx talk, and a few people have written to me to ask me to elaborate more on this point.

If you dissect Steve's vision, it has less to do with being a visionary without limits but one of seeing extreme limits. After all, he was reviving a company with limited room to maneuver. But the limits turned out to be a blessing in disguise. In design, we call it designing with the canvas that you have. The size of it will affect the way you wish to paint a masterpiece. If you see limits as a gift, it will be so.

For example, because Apple had a small PC market share, there was little incentive for distributors to promote its products. That is why Steve decided to enter retail and start Apple stores.

Interestingly, Apple stores are designed with principles similar to those of a cathedral. There is a lot of light, and the architectural features make you look up or draw you in. It is designed differently from a PC marketplace for you to feel the scale to better appreciate and focus on the products.

I was stunned once when I was brought on a tour to the Apple store at Marina Bay Sands in Singapore by an Apple Genius—yes that's what they call staff at any Apple store.

As the escalator reached the top floor and looked out towards a fantastic oculus, the Apple Genius staff said,

"Here you can see this oculus. It is designed like a Roman Catholic Church."

Guided tours provided by staff follow a carefully worded script, as everything is designed by Apple, so it was incredible to hear.

Whether intended to look like cathedrals or not, each Apple store is an architectural wonder. Each one is a sight to behold that holds a lot of value to Apple. In 2017, it was reported that Apple stores have the highest revenue per square foot at $5,546 versus Tiffany & Co. at $2,951. Tim Cook, the CEO of Apple, also shared in 2013 that around 1 million customers visit Apple Stores per day. Not bad for a brand that almost went bankrupt in the late 90s to eventually emerge as one of the most powerful retail brands today.

The lesson to be learned here is that limits are very fertile grounds for breakthrough creativity, and such creativity tends to be more lasting. So, always be welcoming to limits, as it can push you to discover an even better vision.

Stained Glass and Sculptures

No cathedral is complete without beautiful stained glass and sculptures. These aspects often attract people who travel wide and far to visit cathedrals in other towns. So, I ask you: Is your vision's features distinct enough to attract a wider following?

After dealing with the cacophony that comes with a major airport, I was greeted with poise and a warm smile, "Welcome Mr. Chong!'

The kind stewardess is dressed in a green 'kebaya'—a garment worn by women of Southeast Asia. This is Singapore International Airlines, also known as SIA, one of the world's most awarded airlines and one of the few with a long track record of making a profit. The kebaya she is wearing was uniquely designed by Parisian couturier Pierre Alexandre Claudius Balmain in 1974.

Pierre Balmain was an influential designer whose thoughts on fashion were groundbreaking for his time.

He once described the art of dress-making as "the architecture of movement."

His design for the Singapore Stewardess, also known as the Singapore Girl, became so iconic that it became a brand on its own. The woman in the kebaya became so strongly associated with Singapore Airlines that she became a global symbol of great service in the skies and Singapore's vision to the world. Madame Tussaud even chose to use an SIA flight attendant dressed in the blue kebaya to reflect the popularity of international travel.

Looking at SIA's track record seems like a walk in the park. But in its founding years, it was a fragile vision. Without a hinterland to fly to and enormous resources for an airline, there was no clear path for growth; it was an existential battle. Ten months after it was set up in 1972, Lee Kuan Yew told SIA at its inaugural dinner:

> "I set up Singapore Airlines to make profits. If you don't make a profit, I am going to close down the airline."

The management of SIA had only one shot and they had to be bold and to think differently to beat the best in the market. So, the management embodied the mindset that they had to always create extraordinary and world-class experiences. For a smaller airline, the only way to stand out was to be the best.

Even when designing an airline uniform, the management sought out the best to stand out. To provide exceptional food quality rather than canteen food in the air, SIA pioneered the idea of assembling an international cast of chefs to create up-to-date menus, which extended to even those in economy class. As a result, SIA won the Skytrax World Airline Award for best economy-class catering.

In all its endeavors and achievements, SIA brings a good name to the small island state. This means that the airline is like a cathedral that embodies Singapore's vision to deliver a world-class experience. Even before arriving in Singapore, an investor's experience with the country starts by taking an SIA flight.

So, you cannot get a better microcosm of Singapore than through SIA. However, what makes it unique is not something that others cannot achieve. All airlines use the same planes from only one or two manufacturers since the industry is highly regulated, hence, only a select number of suppliers meets the standards.

It is possible to deliver an exceptional experience if any competitor wants to, and SIA has inspired a lot in this regard.

The only difference for SIA is that it has a clear cause and vision for Singapore which empowered the management. This made them work harder to survive by constantly adding unique experiences, the equivalent of stained glass and sculptures to ensure that Singapore Airlines remained unique.

Finding the Master Mason

Would you join a company in free fall, one that is considered near bankruptcy, or any organization that is failing?

Hard to answer, isn't it?

It turns out that there are crazy ones who do. One such person was Tim Cook.

Tim had rejected overtures from Apple recruiters and had a cushy job at Compaq, then the world's largest maker of personal computers (PC). But he decided to meet Steve Jobs because he was the one who created the entire category of personal computing.

In that one fateful conversation after Steve shared his vision and discussed creating an extraordinary product, Tim was hooked and decided to abandon everything and jump ship.

This is an example of what happens when a person is cause-driven and has a clear vision. In other words, a vision is not enough; the person must be able to emanate a clear cause.

Tim was asked in an interview what drew him away from his stable job at Compaq to work for Apple. He said:

"Most of the CEOs I had met were what I think of as 'cufflink' CEOs [...] They're so divorced from and isolated from real people who are working and from the products of the company. And here was this guy who was so animated about the product."

Tim was further questioned why it mattered to him to work for a 'creative genius,' to which he replied:

"It wasn't a Silicon Valley magic kind of sprinkling the dust on you. This guy really wanted to change the world. And I'd never seen that in a CEO before."

Eventually, Tim signed up to be the 'Master Mason' to help Steve Jobs achieve his vision. He fixed the inventory and supply chain issues, and reduced Apple's unsold inventory from one month to two days.

In 2018, Apple became the first US company to reach a market value of US\$ 1 trillion.

The 'Apple Cathedral' under Tim's leadership broke new ground and helped complete Steve's vision for the company.

A Grand Cathedral?
Start with a Blueprint

"I seek to commission the construction of a new cathedral in Tours that will rival the grandeur of Cathédrale Notre-Dame."

- Henri de Marchand

Luminous lights pass through an extensive set of 14th-century windows. It is a marvel to see the cathedral still standing despite being bombed during the Second World War. Its two tall steeples of 157 m high helped guide bombers in raids and have remained standing in a city flattened by Allied bombing.

This is the Cologne Cathedral.

What began as a vision in 1248 took over seven centuries to complete in 1880 with builders being faithful to the original blueprint. The Cathedral, a Gothic masterpiece, is recognized as a UNESCO World Heritage Site.

Before a soaring cathedral is built, it has a blueprint.

In a 1999 YouTube clip, a gentleman named Jack Ma could be seen pitching his blueprint in detail to his 17 friends on how they would bring about a new internet revolution in China. While his friends looked on, perhaps wondering how long the vision would take and whether they could make it, Jack methodically went about his plans confidently in terms of positioning, culture, and approach, and he declared early on:

"Our competitors are not in China but in America's Silicon Valley. So, first we should position Alibaba as a global website!"

This clip has been viewed 2.8 million times and was featured on 60 Minutes, a TV program in the US. Eventually, Alibaba would succeed by leaps and bounds and be listed on the New York Stock Exchange in 2014.

Valued at US$ 167 billion, it was one of the largest IPO offerings in the Exchange's history, and it made Jack, a former English teacher, the richest man in China who saw the possibility of China's e-commerce market rising to rival the US.

He succeeded not just because of hard work. His greatest strength was how holistic he saw the future of Alibaba to be. Like building a cathedral, he could see not just a website but an entire ecosystem. In fact, in the 1999 video, he was prescient in understanding the importance of building a culture to nurture the right talent, critical thinking, and hard work.

Even without knowing how to code, he saw the potential of the industry. More importantly, he articulated his ideas into a clear vision with relatable components that reached out like a cathedral, so it was something that his friends could grasp, especially the part in the video where he said that having a great culture and changing mindsets matter in winning.

Many of his friends who co-founded Alibaba believed in Jack's vision and eventually became extremely wealthy.

Alibaba, or the Alibaba economy, not only changed how small enterprises traded and how consumers bought products in China, but also minted a circle of billionaires, at least 10 of them, with a total net worth of US$ 100 billion. Jack did this by investing directly or partnering with companies that provided services for his online platform, from payment systems to delivery companies. The entire network of Alibaba created a new wealth class whose collective net worth is larger than the economies of 136 countries.

So, if an English school teacher managed to lay out his blueprint for a soaring cathedral of change, what is stopping you?

Visionary Persuasion Can End Empires

Bhagavad gita, a Sanskrit phrase meaning "God's song," is one of the most revered Hindu scriptures. Through these words, Mohandas Karamchand Gandhi, later known as Mahatma Gandhi, found his own spiritual tone and vision, which gave him the strength to lead India's freedom and independence.

But unlike the American Revolution of 1776, Gandhi faced down the largest empire on which the sun never sets, the British Empire, in a creative way.

A lawyer and a seeker of truth, Gandhi was an avid reader of the world's religious texts. He found strength in two Sanskrit words found in the Gita. One was *aparigraha* ("non-possession"), which implies that people must abandon material goods that constrain the life of the spirit and avoid being tied down by money and property.

The next Sanskrit word was Samatvam ("equanimity"), which advocates remaining unruffled by pain or pleasure, victory or defeat, and to work without hope of success or fear of failure.

Inspired by these two principles, Gandhi was fearless. He led the people of India not through armed conflict but through spirituality and a vision of non-violence also known as Ahimsa to reclaim the legitimate rights of the Indian people to determine their own destiny.

He called his vision satyagraha ("Upholding the Truth"), a way to designate a determined but nonviolent resistance to evil. It was an entire philosophy; practitioners of satyagraha taught how to achieve the correct insight into the real nature of an evil situation by observing the non-violence of the mind through seeking truth in a spirit of peace and love. This vision aims to conquer through conversion, not violence, to arrive at a new harmony.

Gandhi preached his vision of satyagraha while being patient and persuasive.

Even though Gandhi was arrested a few times, the attractiveness of his vision could not be stopped. He inspired a national spiritual movement strengthened by his cause and vision to see that eventually the British would not find it tenable to manage this large subcontinent that has turned its back on oppression.

The significant civil disobedience campaigns that he led from 1920–1922, 1930–1934, and 1940–1942, were all well-designed to undermine the moral authorities of the British.

Gandhi's clear arguments about a post-war world where colonies were gaining freedom, the combined firepower of a firm cause, a creative vision for India's future, and a movement of people, led to the people of India gaining independence from the British in 1947. At the time of India's independence, there were about 340 million people.

By emphasizing nonviolence and using his moral authority, Gandhi was able to uniquely influence the whole of India against the country's colonizers without firing a shot. That in itself is a feat and it is how the British lost the crown jewel in the empire—by a movement of nonviolence shaped through vision, patience, and persuasion.

Knowing the Pain and Being Prepared for it

"Use the difficulty."
- Michael Caine, English actor

It is impressive what the human mind can do if it chooses to. I marveled as I looked at old photos of my mom's illustrious career as a performer in the only circus in Singapore. In one photo, she is seen balancing a table with three sheets of plastic between lamps on her nose! A mind-boggling feat. I asked how heavy it was and how long it took for her to train. She said that it was heavy and a bit difficult at first, but after much practice, she overcame it mentally, and then it became easier.

There are growing studies that say that if we lean into negative emotions, it helps us cope better with situations. According to an article in the New York Times in 2023:

"No emotion is inherently bad or inappropriate [...] Anxiety can help you to face a potential threat, anger can help you stand up for yourself and sadness can signal to other people that you need their social support."

- Dr. Emily Willroth, psychologist, Washington University in St. Louis

So instead of avoiding pain and suffering, what happens if we are upfront about it?

When Ernest Shackleton, a famous explorer, was recruiting his team to come along his 1914 Imperial Trans-Antarctic expedition, he did not mince his words on the kind of people he wanted to recruit. The advertisement went like this:

"Men Wanted for Hazardous Journey. Small Wages, bitter cold, long months of complete darkness, constant danger, safe return doubtful. Honor and recognition in case of success."

For the men who knowingly signed on to be part of the expedition in 1915, Shackleton sure did deliver on his promise. The ship for the expedition got stuck early on in pack ice and sank in the Weddell Sea off Antarctica. The crew escaped by coming on the sea ice until it disintegrated, then launched lifeboats to eventually reach the island of South Georgia, barely surviving. By then, they had already endured a stormy ocean voyage of 826.42 miles. The expedition became legendary for resilient leadership in extreme circumstances.

In Walter Issacson's biography of Elon Musk, he wrote that whenever Musk sensed a crisis or a falling back of standards, Musk would call an all-hands-on deck approach to fix the problem. He would be upfront about the crisis, the pain required to overcome the problem, and how long it might take. He would be so transparent that it worried investors, especially in a listed company like Tesla because for them, being so open about problems is not necessarily the way since most companies share good news, not difficulties.

For the many Changemakers who have personally chosen the difficult path towards change, it is important to lay the same stakes before everyone who decides to embark on their journey. So that everyone can also lean in and use the difficulty to meet the scale of the vision before them.

Does Your Cause Drive Your Vision?

On the Netflix show, Asian Comedian Destroys America, comedian Ronny Chieng asked the audience if they knew the slogan of the State of Texas. Someone said, "Lone Star state," another answered, "Don't tread on me," and one said, "Remember the Alamo."

Before Ronny answered, he said that was the vibe the State gave: a no-nonsense approach. Then he went on to answer, "The state motto of Texas is friendship," triggering laughter and applause.

After judging in business and branding awards since 2004, too many vision statements are, comically speaking, very similar to the situation that Ronny described. They are not meant to be guiding principles, and most of them sound like they come from a template by saying things like, "We seek to be the best in class in service and excellence in the industry."

When you further investigate the operations of these companies, it becomes clear why they lack a game-changing strategy or innovation. They are merely focused on survival and profit without a compelling cause to inspire them. This lack of purpose often leads to a stagnant business model and a disengaged workforce. On the other hand, companies with a clear and meaningful cause not only attract customers but also motivate their employees to innovate and strive for excellence.

In an online talk about having purpose organized by Consulus, Lim Boon Heng, Chairman of Temasek Holdings, the investment holding company of the Singapore government, shared an interesting perspective about Lee Kuan Yew who made a very simple yet profound statement on 27 May 1965 in the Malaysian parliament when Singapore was still part of Malaysia. Lee Kuan Yew said:

"My business is the people's happiness."

This one line, which was written into the proclamation of Singapore's independence and the national pledge, defined the cause and vision of Lee. In the 1960s, happiness, for the people of Singapore, meant jobs, housing, education and healthcare.

Lim went on to explain that in the pursuit of the people's happiness by creating jobs, the Singapore government founded a number of enterprises. But soon, when the government realized that it was not the business of regulators to run companies, they set up Temasek to manage these enterprises. The people's happiness is core to Temasek's purpose and everything that the company does is geared towards ensuring that it is maintained.

In 2023, Temasek Holdings managed a portfolio of SG$ 382 billion.

What is the cause that empowers the realization of your vision?

How Do You See Time?

Born out of sheer frustration and tiredness, a CEO asked me, "How long does an exercise about change take on average? How long must I bear with this situation?"

I shared with her that it is not just about the length of time but the phases, and we need to see them as they are.

There are generally 3 phases of change:

1st Phase is Seed: This is where we introduce the vision and framework for success

2nd phase is about Holding Ground: This is when foundational structures and co-anchoring from top-down and bottom-up have to happen to anchor a nascent movement

3rd is Inevitability: Systems are finally in place to constantly seed, groom, train, and scale culture and new behaviors; this then shapes a mature movement for growth and innovation

Just like a cathedral, once the relevant foundations, such as key pillars and walls, are in place, it becomes easier to connect the columns together so that you can eventually place the ceiling on top.

Finally, when a cathedral is up and running, it starts to shape the place's beliefs and economy. Cathedrals were notably built during times of prosperity in Europe and were anchors of great culture and economy.

An interesting case study for this is how Steve Jobs brought change to the smartphone industry.

When he seeded the process, so many in the industry were dismissive. However, he did not just launch a phone. He launched the app store and many other things that laid the foundations for this new approach. Nokia was dominant then, and Steve Ballmer of Microsoft was dismissive of his ideas.

This was in 2007.

During the holding ground phase, everyone started jumping on the bandwagon. Then Google came into the picture with Android in 2008, creating another ecosystem.

Nokia, the once leading mobile phone maker, was sold off to Microsoft in 2013.

By the end of 2017, it became clear who would be the dominant players: Apple and Android. Microsoft exited the smartphone industry in 2017.

All this happened within ten years.

So it is never about how long, but how you shape and make use of your time strategically.

Changemaking Through a Creative Vision

The proof that this is the change you are meant to bring about comes through from the clarity and uniqueness of your creative vision. It starts with being able to sketch out your plans which becomes more apparent as you move along the process of bringing your ideas to life. You may not have the complete picture at the start, but as you progress further, it becomes clearer:

Visualizing the Vision

i. Based on your cause, what is your prophetic vision?

ii. Find your vision from navigating labyrinthine corridors

iii. Will your vision draw others with stained glasses and sculptures?

Building the Vision

iv. Who is your master mason?

v. What is your blueprint?

vi. How do you persuade others with your vision?

Sustaining the Vision

vii.   Preparing your people to face the pain

viii. Ultimately, does your cause drive your vision?

ix.   Not about the length of time but how you see time

As you move along with your vision, one sign that your cause and vision are truly yours is that you will find the unlikely power of attracting talent who will join you, even at great personal cost to themselves.

We will discover this in the next part, Circles of Trust.

PART FOUR: CIRCLE OF TRUST

"Unless I wash your feet, you have no part with me."

Jesus of Nazareth,

Rabbi, Founder of Christianity, Last Supper

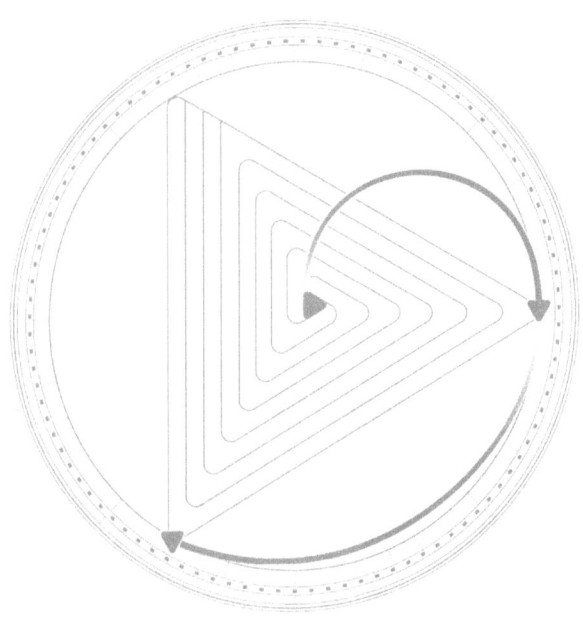

Circle Of Trust

Gathering Your Core

As the sun set, painting the sky with hues of orange and gold across a land of rolling plains and majestic rivers, King Aravind sighed. He wondered if his kingdom, which has enjoyed prosperity and peace, would survive the coming invasion.

"They are here your Majesty," said his mantri or minister.

The King and his mantri then left the palatial opulence and entered the tranquil palace gardens under the ancient banyan tree, which had witnessed the rise and fall of dynasties and empires.

A grand circular table had been set up; King Aravind had gathered his trusted council of generals and advisors, not for counsel but for a meal, a feast rooted in the ancient traditions of Indian hospitality and brotherhood.

Everyone stood up while His Majesty took his seat.

This is not a feast for celebration, so it was devoid of royal luxury. Instead, it was adorned with simplicity and warmth, embodying the essence of dharma and the virtues of the land they were sworn to protect.

Then, in an act deeply rooted in the belief of "Atithi Devo Bhava," which meant the guest is like God, the king personally served each guest their food. This was still an act that deeply surprised the generals and advisors who gathered.

A gesture that touched and moved some to tears, it was an act of service that transcended rank and status, symbolizing the unity required in the face of the adversity ahead.

The meal was vegetarian and prepared with ingredients from the royal gardens. Each dish was imbued with significance—spices for courage, grains for prosperity, and sweets for victory.

After everyone had their fill, King Aravind addressed them:

Men and Women, but above all, my Brothers and Sisters

I have shared a kinship with each of you like a brother, while some of you are like fathers and mothers to me.

We have shared many meals, pains, and joys for the sake of our kingdom.

This coming war is not of our choosing. We have always preferred peace, but the enemy lusts for our land.

I have chosen to serve you as a sign of gratitude to our people. My gesture earlier was not of a King but of a son of this land like you.

As we begin our preparations for war and go into it, I know not if we will see each other.

But I wanted you to know that whatever happens, you mean the world to me and our kingdom.

I would like to present this lamp, lit from the eternal flame that burned in our temple of peace.

Carry this light with you into the darkness we face. Let it remind you of our unity, our cause, and the light within each of us that no shadow can extinguish.

The council left the gardens with renewed spirits, their hearts alight with the flame of unity and purpose.

The battles that followed were fierce. King Aravind died in battle and was succeeded by his daughter.

But the bonds forged under the ancient banyan tree held strong.

The kingdom stood unbroken, a testament to the power of shared conviction and the indomitable spirit of its people.

The tale of King Aravind's meal became a legend, passed down through generations as a parable of leadership, unity, and the sacred bond of trust that turns ordinary men into guardians of their realm.

Essence of Circle of Trust

*"It is infinitely better to have a few
good Men, than many indifferent ones."*

*- President George Washington's letter to James Mchenry,
10 August 1798*

If I asked you to group the people in your life into three tables of inner circles: a table for the cause you believe in, a table of love, and lastly, a table for your interests, who would you have? And how would you group them?

Write their names down and reflect on what each person has gifted you. Certainly, the numbers would be few. The people you have listed are not indifferent to you and they care about who you are and what you do.

I have conducted this exercise in a few keynotes, and it has always been illuminating. Six years ago, when I turned 40, my wife threw me a lovely surprise party. Other than being surprised, I was stunned by the people she thoughtfully invited. It was a small group of close friends from different stages of my life.

Some say that just before someone passes away, one will have a flashback of the people they love and those who matter. In my case, the people in the room would undoubtedly appear in such a flashback. Among that group, I could easily place any of them into my three tables.

Our circles shape us just as we shape them individually. The kind of circles we have has a network effect on the impact we wish to have in the world. No one can change whatever situation we seek to do so alone, even Jesus had his twelve apostles and Winston Churchill had his war cabinet.

The next sign that you are on the right track with your cause and the vision that you have defined is whether you can find the right core circle to build it with you. In the next part, we will explore the effect of this circle of trust in your vision.

But for now, let us look at the people in our circle.

If War Comes, Who Comes to Mind?

There is an organizational chart on paper, another in your head, and one in your heart. In the projects I have worked on, my two favorite questions to leaders are:

In your organization, who will you seek advice from and why?

Then, I will follow up with: Who would you need to have in the room to make difficult calls?

I tend to listen to what kind of counsel these leaders look for to assess the depth of their relationship with whoever is truly the core team. If it is just feedback, it is not of high value but if it is about figuring out a wicked problem, then it is different.

Both questions provide illuminating answers. When it comes to difficult or exceptional situations, there is a hierarchy of persons in mind. That is your inner circle—the circle whom you want to be in your war room.

Here, I want to clarify that these persons may not even be the close friends of the Changemaker, but their counsel makes a difference. Churchill had to manage a war cabinet of diverse interests, some of which were even plotting to take his job towards the end of the war. However, he chose that group because he felt they could move the whole of Britain forward. They earned his trust because their counsel currency is relevant and has mobilization value.

Through this circle of trust, you extend your service and leadership to others. These trusted few are the ones you can lean on and be open about your challenges because the decisions are always complex and hard.

And then the Changemaker will have an even smaller core of trusted colleagues that influences the overall core group.

When going up to a high mountain for a divine encounter, it is said in the Gospels that Jesus only brought Peter, James, and John.

Steve Jobs had Jony Ive and Tim Cook.

Lee Kuan Yew had Goh Keng Swee and S. Rajaratnam.

Having a core group you can trust matters, and until you find these people you cannot influence a wider circle of leaders and motivate them into shaping more circles of influence.

Ultimately, any organization is influenced by a core circle of leaders who, in turn, influence other circles of trust. These circles give feedback and are often overlapping in terms of dynamics and relationship.

Who is Your Mantri?

Facing a somber audience at the Singapore Conference Hall for the State Funeral Service of the late Dr. Goh Keng Swee, who served as Deputy Prime Minister of Singapore on 23 May 2010, Mr Lee Kuan Yew began:

Mr. President,

Ladies and Gentlemen,

It was my good fortune to have strong men around me. Of all my Cabinet colleagues, it was Goh Keng Swee who made the greatest difference to the outcome for Singapore. He had a capacious mind and a strong character. When he held a contrary view, he would challenge my decisions and make me re-examine the premises on which they were made. As a result, we reached better decisions for Singapore.

*In the middle of a crisis, his analysis was always sharp, with
an academic detachment and objectivity that reassured me.
His robust approach to problems encouraged me to press on
against seemingly impossible odds.*

In Sanskrit, *mantri* means sage.

In every circle of trust, there is one person with whom
you discuss critical ideas and possible scenarios to determine
your next course of action. In the early days of founding independent Singapore, Goh Keng Swee was the mantri for Lee
Kuan Yew.

Many people worldwide may have heard about Lee, but
not enough about Goh. However, within Singapore, he has
been widely acknowledged as the architect of modern Singapore, coming up with ingenious ideas for the island state to
survive and thrive. Not only was he wise in his counsel, but he
also proved to be the right-hand man of the Prime Minister
by setting up several key government offices and initiatives.

For a fledgling island nation, Singapore had to be creative
in its nation-building approach because there was no benchmark to follow. To build the economy, Goh set up the Economic Development Board (EDB) to attract investors to set
up shop in Singapore. At that time, there was no concept of
globalization yet, but Goh and Lee determined early to place
their bets on serving the global economy. Until today, the
same EDB that Goh instituted remains a critical pillar in the

economic success of Singapore and oversaw US$158 billion worth of foreign direct investment into Singapore in 2023.

He even converted swampland into an industrial park despite critics doubting his vision. Eventually, the Singapore model of industrial parks would be adopted by China, initially through the Suzhou Industrial Park Project, and then throughout the country. Vietnam and Indonesia also adopted this model.

His insights and advice were so highly sought after, that upon retirement, the Chinese government appointed him to study and advise on the development of coastal economic zones.

He was truly a sage of his time. In striving for change, who is your mantri?

THREAD 42

Harness the Virtues of the Land
to Bind a Kingdom

When wars cannot be placated, natural disasters like famine, disrupt the harmony in the kingdom. When this happens, the emperor can be ousted.

This is called the 'Mandate of Heaven,' also known as Tian Ming, which was invoked by the Zhou Dynasty (1045–256 BC) to justify overthrowing the previous Shang Dynasty. This concept is so ingrained in the 13 major dynasties in the history of China that even conquest dynasties believed in and tried to adhere to these principles.

Conquest dynasties refer to emperors who are not ethnically of the Han race (the majority of people in China are ethnic Han), like the Mongols, who ruled China during the Yuan Dynasty (1279–1368) and then the Qing Dynasty, the last dynasty of China from 1644–1911. The Qing Dynasty was by a race from the northeast known as the Manchu people.

The general idea of the Mandate of Heaven defines the principles of trust between the ruler and the ruled in China, so it means that whether you are Han or non-Han, so long as you are delivered, you can rule. Until today, the principles of the Mandate of Heaven, which held one of the world's largest civilizations together, still matters in Communist China.

On the other hand, Europe, another ancient civilization that has also faced centuries of bloodshed, follows a different set of principles.

For a continent composed of strong empires in different moments of history, from the Romans to the Spanish to the Austro-Hungarian empires, the creation of a supranational structure known as the European Union was no easy feat.

It did so because of shared human, cultural, and spiritual values that defined what it means to be European.

As a concept and as an idea for people, the European Union is rightly called a sui generis political entity as it has both a federation and a confederation within it. There were fears that Brexit could have triggered its dismantling, but it did not. Furthermore, Russia's invasion of Ukraine has very much strengthened the idea of a stronger EU.

"Pour que l'Union européenne fonctionne, la compétition qui stimule, la solidarité qui unit, la coopération qui renforce."

(A Europe built on competition that stimulates, cooperation that strengthens, and solidarity that unites.)

- Jacques Delors, the architect of the united Europe in an Address to the European Parliament, 19 January 1995

Today, the European Union covers a total area of 1,707,642 mi^2 and an estimated total population of over 448 million. Its GDP is estimated to be $19.35 trillion or one-sixth of the global economy.

From these examples, I hope to illustrate that there are indeed opportunities to creatively harness common virtues to bind a diverse group into a shared circle.

Kingship Through Service

A victorious general, who had every right to claim the spoils of war and power, was suspected by his enemies of seeking to declare himself King of the New Republic. This general strode into the statehouse at Annapolis, Maryland, filled with members of Congress, and declared:

> *"Having now finished the work assigned me, I retire from the great theatre of Action—and bidding an Affectionate farewell to this August body under whose orders I have so long acted, I here offer my Commission, and take my leave of all the employments of public life."*

> *- George Washington, General & Commander in Chief of the Army of the United Colonies, December 23, 1783*

He then bowed and surrendered his military commission to an inspired and grateful congress of the newly independent United States of America. With this heroic act, he returned to his farm.

When American artist Benjamin West told King George III of England that George Washington would choose to resign, the King who had lost the thirteen colonies said,

"If he does that, he will be the greatest man in the world."

Indeed, the greatest test of any person is what he or she would do with absolute power. Too many chose to use power for themselves: Julius Caesar, Mao Zedong, and Joseph Stalin, to name a few famous examples.

George Washington had absolute power but chose to serve under a great cause and assembly. But this was not the end.

George Washington would later be asked to return to serve as the first president, a position not of absolute power but that of service to hold the fragile unity of the states together and shape the key foundations of a young nation for posterity. At the same time, he did this with a circle of leaders who were not the easiest to handle because they had diverse views and were powerful in their own right.

He could have used his past sacrifices to overrule them but he chose to serve with moral authority and steer the young nation's development. One example of this was the months of intense debate about the United States Constitution. One person involved in the process, James Monroe, summed up the role of George Washington to Thomas Jefferson in a letter saying:

"Be assured, [Washington's] influence carried the government."

Eventually, the Constitution was written and passed. After serving two terms as President of the United States, George Washington stepped down willingly according to the Constitution of the young nation. In his farewell speech, he implored his fellow citizens to unite:

"The name of American, which belongs to you in your national capacity, must always exalt the just pride of patriotism more than any appellation derived from local discriminations. With slight shades of difference, you have the same religion, manners, habits, and political principles. You have, in a common cause, fought and triumphed together. The independence and liberty you possess are the work of joint councils and joint efforts—of common dangers, sufferings, and successes."

- George Washington, First President of the United States of America, September 1796

The Power of Kinship

"We work together around a kitchen table. We have our lives all around the products. In some ways it feels like a small company. We'll sit there with our sketch books and trade ideas. That's where the really hard, brutal honest criticism comes in."

- Christopher Stringer, Apple Industrial Designer in his testimony as expert witness in the Patent Trial of Apple versus Samsung, 2012

In the legal case of Samsung versus Apple on design infringement, both companies had to present their design processes and cultures. The testimony above was shared during the blockbuster trial.

Samsung had hundreds more designers but a spirit of distrust and fear prevailed. On the other hand, while Apple had only 17 core designers, they managed to establish a circle of trust where they could discuss ideas around a kitchen table and were comfortable critiquing each other.

If you were to measure the value of this trusted core and the impact of their work on Apple, you would know that the kinship of these designers is valuable and a key contributor to turn Apple into a business with a US$ 2 trillion market value.

In 2016, a groundbreaking study by Google shed insights into what makes a perfect team. The study revealed that it is not those with the best minds or resources but those that can shape a psychologically safe space that recognizes divergent thinking and is comfortable with critique.

Having said this, for kinship to be of value, it has to be done intentionally by design. The team at Apple are professionals and competent in their skills who bring different perspectives to the table, so it is not the case of bringing random people into the fold.

To nurture valuable kinship by design, there is a need to use what I coin the "Garden Theory for Unity" approach. Here are three fundamental principles or the 3Ds of this concept:

1. Divergent reality

As one can imagine, a garden has to be diverse to be beautiful. It should have large trees, small shrubs, and flower beds, but must all come together to form a visual feast. However, a garden also requires careful nurturing; it is fragile and every plant requires a different approach.

Accepting divergent reality means being open to differing ideas and intentionally designing the participation process to give everyone a stake in it.

2. Design intentionally

A garden will always be a work in progress and the task of building unity is no different. It takes a long time to shape a garden because it is fragile and can be easily destroyed.

To design intentionally means that everyone has to be clear on the cause and seek ways to design solutions to solve it without getting personal.

3. Dialogue always

Just like a garden needs dedicated cultivation for diverse plants, you also need dedicated forums, processes, and good institutions to deepen understanding, nurture shared views, and continuously seed the value of each other's ideas and development.

Through these principles, you can shape the kind of kinship that changes the world.

Summon the Courage
to Move Any Army

With the morning sun beating down on us like a sauna blanket, we marched off. It was going to be a long day as around 400 of us were participating in a military parade in Sumatra, Indonesia. I was walking alongside my men when, suddenly, we were told to halt. I moved up to the front since I was the platoon sergeant to see what was happening.

The spot on the parade square where we were supposed to be standing was marked with the name of our army unit, now occupied by a unit of the other military we were having a joint exercise with, the Tentara Nasional Indonesia, or Indonesian Armed Forces.

Warrant Officer Mani, my Regimental Sergeant Major, a Napoleon-sized Indian man, walked up to the Indonesian Army Contingent, who towered over him. With a smile, he politely said in Malay that they were in the wrong spot.

They ignored him, and so we were in a standoff. You could hear the trees rustle nearby and sweat droplets forming on our brows. No one moved. The only difference in this standoff is that you have young Singaporean boys who are green behind the ears and were there because of compulsory national service versus full-time servicemen of the Indonesian Army who have seen combat. A classic boys versus men situation.

He asked again, this time clearer, by indicating that their position was right next to ours. Again, no one moved.

Then Officer Mani walked over to our sign and said loudly, "Since this must be a mistake, then this sign is pointless." He then took up our sign and threw it to the ground.

The Indonesian contingent then moved immediately!

I have thought about this episode many times in my life. If war did come, I would follow an officer like Mani. Why did the Indonesian contingent move? My own conclusion is that courage will make you equal to any power.

More importantly, Officer Mani taught me the courage to speak truth to power and to summon courage in the face of injustice.

I thought about what was happening in his head at that time and what gave him certainty. This instance helped me many times whenever I was afraid, to remind myself that if I am clear about my cause, then I should dare to ask, summon, and say what must be said.

We may not need to face real military battles. But there are other kinds of battles that require us to fight, to take a stand, to speak the truth, and to lead others in hard decisions.

I experienced this in another instance when we were working on bringing change to Wenzao Ursuline University of Languages in Kaohsiung. After finishing the two-month strategic study, we presented two strategies for the university's leadership. One was an improvement on the current state of the institution, and the other option was more ambitious. Everyone voted but it was split down the middle.

Then the President of the University at that time, Margaret, said, "If I believe in the more ambitious path and I take personal responsibility, will you all follow me? This is Wenzao, this is about the heart of our values, and it is important. Will you all come with me?"

There was silence but everyone knew that she had put her job on the line, so everyone chose the most ambitious one.

Sadly, cowardice is more common than courage. But every time I get the chance to witness courage, it is always a privilege of a lifetime, and it is what sparks an entire movement to action.

A Lamp That Lights Up the Darkness

"For her work for bringing help to suffering humanity."

- The brief citation of the Nobel Peace Prize 1979
that was awarded to Mother Teresa

When the world's most famous nun of Albanian descent, an Indian Citizen, died on 5 September 1997, her passing became a world event. Against the usual protocol, the Indian government decided to accord her a state funeral, which is usually reserved only for presidents and prime ministers, where a moment of national mourning would be observed.

Her funeral, attended by a million people, Kings, Queens, Presidents, and Prime Ministers, became a historic moment as the world sent off the "Saint of the Gutters."

However, Mother Teresa's cause did not end with her death. By the time she died, the movement she founded, the Missionaries of Charity, consisting of women who chose to follow the path of poverty and chastity, became an indomitable force with nearly 4,000 nuns. Some men even followed Mother Teresa's movement while others became Catholic priests. There was also a growing number of international volunteers who served everywhere.

By 1997, the Missionaries of Charity ran 517 orphanages, hospices, homes for people experiencing poverty, and other charity centers in 123 nations.

Mother Teresa, however, did not leave her movement leaderless. Prior to her death, she tried to step down twice. But it was only in the last year of her life that the leadership within the Missionaries of Charity agreed. Through an 8-week selection process, the group elected Sr. Nirmala Joshi to take her place.

It was clear from day one that Mother Teresa was a Changemaker with a game plan to ensure lasting change. She was astute enough to carefully define the structures of her cause so that the light she discovered could be passed on properly long after her death.

What Mother Teresa had done is not unique in the Catholic Church. Throughout different periods, especially dark moments within the church, many Catholics have felt called to bring about change in a particular way. They are believed to have received a "charism" that is defined as a special light from God that results in a lasting movement to serve as a channel of His goodness for people.

Throughout the two thousand year history of the Catholic Church, many saints have received this special light who subsequently created lasting movements to change the church and the world. In fact, when a few Popes were lost, saints such as Francis of Assisi and Catherine of Siena helped light their paths.

Another famous saint who changed the church and the world is Jean-Baptiste de La Salle, who founded a religious movement called the La Salle Brothers in the 17th century. They run one of the largest school systems in the world. As of 2023, the religious order consists of 3,000 Brothers who live in communities and run 1,100 education centers in 80 countries with more than a million students.

Finding your cause and seeing a creative vision is not enough. It is important to be astute in setting up the structures to carefully define the light that will continue to be passed onto others to illuminate the darkness and continue the cause for a long time.

"If I ever become a Saint—I will surely be one of "darkness". I will continually be absent from Heaven—to light the light of those in darkness on earth."

- Mother Teresa, from the book "Come be my light"

How Many Hearts Do You Need
to Ignite for Change?

One favorite question I get from leaders is: "How many people do I need to make change happen?"

What do you think?

In my experience with Consulus, it is never the number but the type of people you need to ignite and shape change.

In any organization, you will have shapers, doers, and coordinators.

Shapers are those who feel the calling. They are the exceptional few who are constantly able to see the big picture and help shape organizations. You can call them leaders, but they are not only leaders in name.

Then there are leaders with grand titles who fit the category of doers. These people are not necessarily shapers, especially if they do not know how to see inward and can only see problems, not pathways.

Then you have the coordinators, who are shaped by the shapers' vision. In a recent discussion about how many civil servants in the United Kingdom ran the British empire in the 19th century, a ridiculously low number was mentioned: about 40,000, according to the National Archives of the U.K.

Of course, these do not include the local officials in all the colonies, but still, this group that we consider as the coordinators is low by any standard. This is even more fascinating if you consider that this was at the height of the British empire, which is the largest in world history.

In 1913, 412 million people were part of the British Empire, estimated to be about 23% of the world's population. The empire stretched from east to west, covering a huge land mass of 13.71 million square miles, about a quarter of the world's land area. This is why the tagline, "where the sun never sets," stuck with the British Empire.

If you extend this idea to religion, just in the Catholic Church alone, which has 1.3 billion members in 2023, there are only 5,340 bishops who are leaders of local circles or dioceses. And when it comes to priests, there are less than half a million. Then there is another significant group called the missionaries and religious congregations which is estimated to be around 600,000.

Another example is, if you review any elected government representation, the ratio of elected representatives to the population remains very low. According to the Pew Research

Center in 2017, the U.S. House of Representatives had one voting member for every 747,000 Americans.

Truly cause-driven leaders who have a concrete creative vision and are able to hold together different circles of trust are the real shapers.

In Steve Jobs and George Washington's case, shapers are those who were selected into their core team.

If you go by numbers alone, only a few people are shapers. The number of coordinators is composed of a manageable size, too. As I shared earlier, if Changemakers, who genuinely embody the characteristics of a shaper, have found their cause, there is no doubt that they can move mountains.

Now back to the question of how many people you need to make change happen. The formula is actually closer to this:

To ignite and sustain change, it is critical for a focused 1% of shapers to positively influence another 1% of coordinators, thereby initiating a chain reaction that eventually impacts about 20-30% of doers or enthusiatic followers and this is already enough to drive change.

The Bonds Forged Under a Banyan Tree

The Banyan tree or *Akshay Vat* is considered a tree with no end because it has a lifespan of up to 500 years. The complex weave of branches, leaves, and roots descend like string curtains from the branches into the ground, eventually becoming trunks. Its thick canopy does not allow sunlight to pass through, thus making it ideal as shade and clear ground for gathering. It is such a majestic and imposing tree that it has long been revered by Hindus and Buddhists. Lord Buddha attained enlightenment by sitting under the shade of the Akshay Vat.

Just like this tree, the bonds of a group of changemaking leaders are forged over time that goes beyond simply working together. There needs to be special moments of what I call "Banyaning" together, initiated by the lead or founding Changemaker to reflect and deepen their understanding of a situation to forge lasting bonds.

Steve Jobs was famous for his different encounters with the key staff of Apple. Although a lot of it is kept a secret, one or two have been shared on the Internet such as his view of the PC world and what Apple needs to do. He believes that work is not just about doing but knowing the purpose, and then building on that to shape the work.

One of the most famous videos uploaded probably by someone from Apple on YouTube was a small staff meeting held on 23 Sept 1997. The video begins with Steve by framing the effort behind reviving Apple and mentions that "Apple has pockets of greatness and has somehow drifted away." This helped focus his audience and internal staff on what truly mattered. He then proceeded to say what he believes is unnecessary and what is needed for Apple to thrive in the future and revealed that an astounding 70% of the product line had been chopped, making clear the stakes at hand. Further, he indicated the path towards customer-centric innovation in the future.

Immediately after, he took a pause and went on a deepening discussion of his worldview about the way the Apple brand is communicated and what needs to change. He also discussed his reflections of society and how, in a noisy world, the focus should be on values and not the products. For Steve, Apple is not about making boxes for people to get their jobs done, saying,

"We believe that people with passion can change the world for the better."

This became known as the moment Steve helped bring his key team with him to change the world.

Let us revisit what he did that constituted Banyaning:

First, he did the **deepening** phase. He presented his worldview to deepen their understanding of what should matter to the core team.

Second, he went on toward the **dividing** phase. He drew the lines and created the chasm to nudge the team to pick a clear side by clearly presenting the stakes.

Third, he defined the **calling**, where he helped everyone see his vision and the direction where they were headed. This set the pace for Apple's meteoric rise.

As a Changemaker, when was the last time you experienced a Banyaning moment?

Conviction by Design to Fuel
an Indomitable Spirit

Sounds of galloping horses were quickly followed by a command to the 40,000 soldiers in tents. On the Emperor's orders, every soldier shall paint the symbol of the cross on every shield before marching into battle.

For the average Roman soldier, the cross is associated with capital punishment. Crucifixion is a cruel process that is done in public to instill fear and secure authority for the empire. For the last 300 years, the cross has also been associated with the small Christian cult that Roman emperors have persecuted, so the order should be bewildering on many levels.

Staring at the massive wall painting of the Battle of Milvian Bridge in the Hall of Constantine of the Vatican Museum, these were the thoughts in my head. This battle, where Emperor Constantine was said to have seen a sign in heaven of the cross and used it as his labarum, or his military standard into battle, changed history in more ways than one. Constantine was battling the other Roman Emperor for supremacy in 312. When he won the battle, the following year, in 313, Constantine issued the Edict of Milan, which made Christianity an officially recognized and tolerated religion in the Roman Empire.

The year 312 marked the beginning of the Emperor and the empire's conversion into the Christian faith. Before this, with the ongoing persecution of Christianity, there was no sign that the Christians were significant in numbers or influential enough to bring about this kind of change.

The conversion of the Roman Empire to Christianity marked a seismic shift in Western civilization. One of the most brutal empires in history changed in quick succession from violence to adopting a message of love. Out of reverence to Jesus, the most famous victim of crucifixion, Constantine the Great, the first Christian Emperor, abolished crucifixion in the Roman Empire in 337. Jesus the Nazarene, accused of claiming to be king to challenge Roman rule, was estimated to have been crucified in 33 AD. About 300 years after his death, his followers, through no violent attempt to overthrow the empire, managed to convince many to follow in his spirit.

What is so exceptional about this Christian cult since the Romans tolerated all sorts of religions? Other than not yielding to worshiping other gods, the other distinction of the Christian religion that sets it apart from other religious beliefs is its ability to self-organize according to a set of principles over a long period of time.

Despite countless persecutions and the killing of hundreds of leaders, the Christian faith managed to re-emerge and kept propagating the same Christian belief through stories, even without a fixed written form. The official canon of books for the Christian bible that we are familiar with today was not finalized as a code until 397 AD.

It was the passing down of traditions and stories around a trusted circle of leaders who found many creative ways to keep their communities together and connected that kept the group going for over 300 years and made it resilient.

In the exercises that I integrate in my work with organizations, I often present a framework about organizing conviction to be a resilient force for longevity, called **The Nine Dimensions**.

First, to shape a lasting organization, you need to focus on the **Leadership Dimension** which consists of three relational aspects. It begins with the founder, who gathers a circle of leaders, who then continues to keep a larger circle of trust with disciples.

However, to sustain the evolution of the organization, there needs to be a constant deepening and evolving of beliefs. This is where the **Beliefs Dimension** comes into play. This also consists of three relational aspects. Here, a cause which is initially an inspiring spark, is defined as a code of governance, which then needs to become a full system that guides the faithful to be in line with the cause.

Lastly an organization will be severely tested, so this last pillar, the **Evolution Dimension** composed of three related aspects will matter. Any community begins with an inspired way of doing things which needs to be studied, eventually becoming thought leadership. To sustain relevance of thinking, it has to be constantly reviewed for feedback and improvement for longevity.

Through this framework, the organization is able to relate back to the cause, keep the community together, and constantly evolve to meet present-day challenges.

Circles of Trust for Changemaking

No one can ignite change alone, especially if we want to inspire and mobilize a movement. But that can only happen once we have a trusted core to shape the movement with us. So, as an outward circular movement of influence, you should evaluate your strategies using this framework:

Find your core circle

i.   If war comes, who will you call?

ii. Who is your key right hand person or your Mantri?

iii. What are the virtues that unite your group?

How does your core circle relate with one another?

iv. Who are you willing to serve?

v.   Does your kinship allow critique?

vi. Does this core team have courage?

Will your core hold the movement together?

vii. What is the light that you can pass on?

viii. Who is the 1% that ignites the next 1%?

ix.   Is your conviction done systematically by design?

Not all of us can find a movement quickly. The key is having a trusted core circle that will serve as your cornerstone. The next step is assessing whether the talent you have attracted has the commitment and competency to drive change in concrete ways.

"It is in the character of growth that we should learn from both pleasant and unpleasant experiences."

Nelson Mandela, South African anti-apartheid activist, first black president of South Africa from 1994 to 1999

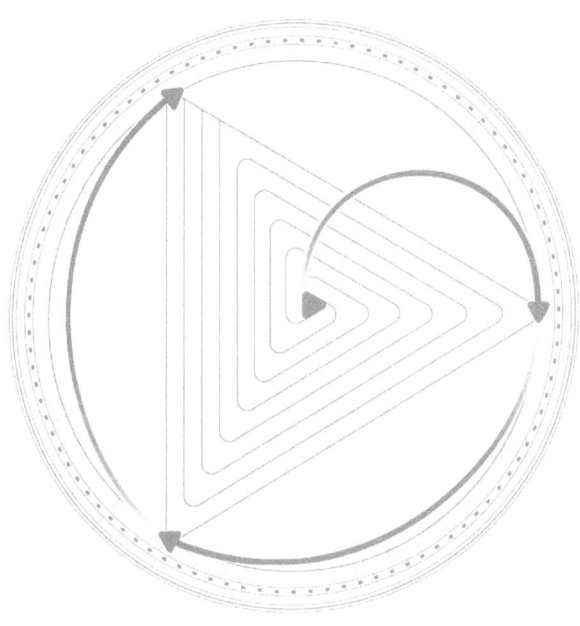

The Butterfly Pivot

Transfiguration

With sunlight shining everywhere, the meadow is an array of colors. It's another beautiful day as Olivia munches on delicious green leaves. A curious one, her favorite pastime is to pause and marvel at the insects that can fly, like beetles and butterflies. As a caterpillar, she felt that flying was beyond her.

Suddenly, a large butterfly flapped its wings next to the leaf she was on, and she nearly fell off it.

"Careful, dear, your days of dreaming about flying can get to you," said a wise old ladybug that landed beside Olivia.

Olivia replied, "I know, but how I long to be able to fly." Surprised, the wise old ladybug said, "Didn't they tell you that it is your destiny to be like them, a butterfly?"

Olivia's eyes sparkled with delight, "Really? No, I did not know that."

"Well then, you better get prepared, as your turn will come soon. Talk to one of them about the experience because they were all once like you, creepy crawlers before becoming fairies of the garden, said the ladybug who then took off.

Olivia was suddenly driven and taken by the realization that her destiny was to be a butterfly. Among all the butterflies in the meadow, she admired Francesca the most. She had the most beautiful wings that looked almost like the rainbow and shimmered with gold-like features.

She decided to summon her courage the next time she would see Francesca fly by.

At this moment, Francesca, fluttering beautifully above her, asked, "How are you, Olivia?

"Francesca, oh, how I longed to speak with you. The wise ladybug has told me that my destiny is to join you in the skies. Please tell me how it happened to you," said Olivia.

Francesca replied, "Well, for me, it was a surprise as well. One moment we were crawling so slowly only to find out the next moment that we could fly as high as we could. It is quite a lot to take in. But the process in itself requires a lot of losing of oneself."

"Losing? What do you mean?"

"One moment, we were eating and going about our business. Soon, our bodies will tell us that we need to rest, not just any rest, but a very long rest. And you will know this moment because you start to have special abilities, too. So, you cannot be afraid but follow your intuition. This intuition will play a big part in your transformation," Francesca explained.

"So, when I had this sensation, I had to have this long rest. I had the knowledge to know where to lean on, and I had this ability to spin a silk cocoon around me when it formed like a small pod for me to rest in its entirety without disturbances."

Then Francesca directed Olivia to look in a specific direction, "Do you see those silk pods? They are like us, waiting to be butterflies."

Olivia asked what happened inside the pod to which Francesca replied, "Well, as I went into this long sleep, I realized that I had no more control over my body; I was losing the ability to move, but I had to trust that this was the right process. After a long while, I do not know how long, I felt this incredible urge and surge of energy to extend my limps. I did, and I broke out of my cocoon, but as I was afraid to fall, I decided to use all my energy to arrest my fall. That was when I realized I had wings and I could fly; it was the most unforgettable experience ever."

"Wow, what a miracle! You just trusted in the process to eventually fly," remarked Olivia.

"That is a nice way of putting it. Anyway, I got to go, but your turn will come soon enough. I will see you in the air someday, sister," said the butterfly and flew away.

Since that day, Olivia munched and crawled with a lot more purpose. She understood her destiny and knew that she had to trust with all her heart that it would all be well.

One morning, just like any other day in the beautiful meadow, Olivia basked in the warm glow of the sun. Still, she felt a strange sensation coursing through her body. Her skin began to tighten, and she knew her time had come. With a sense of wonder and hope, she spun that silver thread around herself and nestled in her turn to sleep in the cozy cocoon.

Inside the silky cocoon, Olivia underwent a profound metamorphosis. Her body dissolved into a soupy mixture of cells, while imaginal discs, dormant since her birth as a caterpillar, sprang to life. Slowly, in a process that felt like choreographed movements, these discs orchestrated the formation of wings, antennae, and other butterfly features.

Many moons passed, and Olivia lay in a deep sleep, patiently waiting for this transformation to come into being. One glorious morning, with the warm sun on her cocoon, she felt an immediate urge to extend herself.

She broke free with a burst of energy, although worried about falling, and took flight immediately. Suddenly realizing she could fly, Olivia flapped her wings as mightily as she could to rise above the meadows; there, she saw the other butterflies.

She soon found Francesca and glided towards her. As sunlight danced on her iridescent wings of orange and gold, she felt so free to explore the boundless skies.

A new adventure now awaits.

Essence of Competent Pivot

"Survival is the ability to swim in strange water."

- Frank Herbert, Author of Dune

A group of astronauts were sent as explorers from Earth. After a near-light-speed space voyage, about 300 light years from the solar system, they landed on a planet similar to Earth but soon noticed a strange phenomenon. Here, humans are primitive while apes are the advanced species controlling military force and science.

This, by the way, is the plot of the 1968 movie Planet of the Apes, but still a very accurate reflection of the evolution of the human race.

Scientifically speaking, we descended from apes, and happen to be very special simians. Though humans are not descended from any monkey or primate living today, we share the same ancestry. But human evolution has been extraordinary, similar to the transformation of a caterpillar into a butterfly.

Human beings have also shown extraordinary ability to adapt to different climates. From Everest to the Arctic to the Sahara, our bodies have evolved over centuries to adapt to extreme climates.

Another extraordinary gift that human beings possess is the ability to use our minds to create magnificent tools that can bring us into space. In principle, to pivot and adapt competently is deeply human, it is what sets us apart from our ancestral cousins. The only way to drive change is to welcome it and shape the new world.

We will explore in more depth in the next chapter how new futures might shape the world.

For now, let us competently pivot to meet the future.

Getting a Grip on Fleeting Change

Peering out of a glass dome, one can see the city in all its glory. It feels as if I have just landed in a spaceship and am about to explore a new planet. But no, this is no sci-fi movie; I am here in the Gardens by the Bay Dome. The dome is a spanking new greenhouse enclosure that houses all the world's species of plants. This artificially constructed structure is another future casting project quintessential in Singapore. Besides Dubai and Shanghai, only some cities can match this island state's breakneck speed of progress.

Growing up here means being comfortable in the displacement and movement of recognizable landmarks, streets, and the skyline. This is an impatient city.

It almost feels like Singapore, a former British colony, has to constantly outpace others in progress in order to justify its purpose and existence. After gaining independence, the government tore down many vestiges of the 'empire' and built up its own vision of the world—a vibrant and modern metropolis.

Change is all around us and in the age of AI, we can see its immediate effect in real-time through likes, posts, and many dings of messages which is now also feeding machine learning at scale. Information and transactions happen 24 hours a day, and it is a complex process that can raise new fortunes, erase the savings of millions in an instant, and misappropriate our likeness to do things that we did not consent to.

As a city-state, Singapore has rapidly risen as one of the tiger economies in Asia from the 70s onwards. It is the first global city to host F1's night race, which is an apt representation of its pursuit of breakneck success.

Singapore excels at being the first in many things. This is one of the first nations to vaccinate the majority of its population during the COVID-19 pandemic and one of the first to open up to the world.

Being first is in the DNA of a Singaporean.

However, growing up in such a city has a downside. Schools were certainly not helpful in making people understand Singapore's pace and movement. In gaining speed, the country did not have the patience for questions or critical thinking. One is expected to simply trust the enlightened view of political leadership. Today, the situation has improved, but during my time, it's either you conform or be reduced to nothing.

Growing up here is less about dreams and more about fitting the ambition of the nation. I remember feeling down when I accompanied my sister to her school's parent-teacher meeting since my dad had to work, and my mom, who did not have a chance to go to school, barely understood English. The teacher showed a chart that depicted the flow of life as a linear process of school and then simply: work. In other words, life is not about mission or purpose. We go to school to learn only to become employees in a capitalist society.

And yet only when I was deep in the work of changemaking globally, and I looked back at Singapore, did I realize how fortunate I was. Circumstances did not lend Singapore a good hand. In 1965, after breaking away from Malaysia, there was no playbook for an island state only slightly larger than Manhattan without resources, where even basic water supply was on a negotiated lease.

Yet, at the height of the Brexit debate in the United Kingdom, the former colonial masters of the island state stated that their vision was to be another Singapore. What a strange turn of events! The past ruler of an empire that once proclaimed the sun would never set to one day claim one of its tiniest former colonies as a benchmark of progress instead of, say, Australia, which until today recognizes King Charles as its sovereign.

The key is to not fear even when change seems fleeting or beyond our reach. There is a method to the chaos happening around us. But the first step we must take is not to worry but to fearlessly seek to break things down and rebuild them in our favor.

From Creepy Crawlers to Flying Fairies

Metamorphosis is one of the most dramatic changes that can happen in nature. About 75% of known insects develop in four stages: egg, larva, pupa, and adulthood. What is most significant, however, is how different the larva looks and behaves from the adult. Certainly, the most stunning metamorphosis is that of a caterpillar transforming into a winged art form. Scientists are still trying to understand the benefits and reasons for such transformations.

However, we can argue that nature has taught us that the purpose of constant evolution in any species is survival. This applies to anything in the world, too. Whether an organization or government will survive depends on how well they evolve in their models and find ways to increase their odds for survival.

In Consulus' 20 years of work for change with individuals and organizations, we have seen that one can achieve four possible pivots.

First is Related Pivot: This is about building on your core capabilities and moving up in the value chain.

Second is Asymmetrical Pivot: This is about evolving your core capabilities and entering into a field related to your current industry.

Third is the Experiential Pivot: This is about entering into a field that is highly experience-based and changes your engagement with stakeholders.

Fourth is Disruptive Pivot: The last one is the ultimate; it is about pivoting through high leadership development or innovation in delivering sophisticated value that entrenches your leadership with deep skill sets.

There is a famous legend about what started the long-standing feud between Lamborghini and Ferrari in the 1960s. At that time, Ferruccio Lamborghini made his money from building tractors for farmers, while Enzo Ferrari made his money from building race cars for the rich and famous.

One day, Ferruccio, who owned a Ferrari, found that the clutches kept giving him problems and needed constant repair at the Ferrari factory. Frustrated, he got his mechanics, who built tractors, to take a look. His men reported that Ferrari was using the same clutch component as what Lamborghini uses for its tractors but was charging 1000 lire for the same part. Furious about this, he confronted Enzo Ferrari himself.

"Ferrari, your cars are rubbish!" said Ferruccio.

To which Enzo replied, "You may be able to drive a tractor, but you will never be able to handle a Ferrari properly."

"This," Ferruccio Lamborghini later was alleged to have said, "was the point where I finally decided to make a perfect car."

This account was never verified, though Ferruccio was alleged to have fanned it himself.

But whether it was true or false, what is factual is that Ferruccio did set up a car factory to design a high-speed luxurious car because he possessed the core engineering skills. So, the approach was not beyond him. It was more of the perception in the initial years of whether a tractor company could succeed in making racer cars. Today, when the word Lamborghini is mentioned, there is no doubt of its power and status. I am sure you will find it unbelievable that it started as a tractor company.

What Ferruccio applied in this case was both an asymmetrical and an experiential pivot simultaneously.

During the company's 50th anniversary, the one-model-only Lamborghini Egoista, the most expensive Lamborghini, was produced. It is valued at a remarkable $117 million and sits in the Lamborghini Museum in Sant'Agata Bolognese.

So, yes, just like a butterfly's metamorphosis, creepy crawlers can become flying fairies.

Losing Oneself to Find New Pivots

"Knowing How to Lose" was the title of a book written by Chiara Lubich, and it disturbed me greatly because in Singapore, we hate losing. So, learning how to lose and not to win was hard for me in the beginning, but later on in life, I saw its wisdom.

Unless we let go, we cannot move on. Unless we lose the pride of our knowledge, we cannot receive new learnings.

The name China, in Chinese (中国, Zhōngguó), literally means "center of the world." The first map in history that truly showed China as the center of the world was done by Mandarin scholars in collaboration with an Italian missionary, Matteo Ricci.

The map was commissioned by Ming Emperor Wanli in 1602, who was impressed by Matteo's command of the Chinese language and writing. He was the first European invited to enter the Forbidden City at the invitation of the Emperor.

The map, known as 坤舆万国全图 or Map of the Ten Thousand Countries of the Earth, achieved several firsts. It brought together China and the West's knowledge of their respective known worlds. It was on this map that America was first revealed to the Chinese and greatly expanded their worldview.

It was also a project done out of mutual respect. Matteo did not do it under duress, nor did he preach the superiority of Western know-how to the Chinese. It was because of his willingness to lose even his identity with the West to enter the East, that gained the confidence of Chinese rulers.

Matteo Ricci is a Christian Missionary whose aim was the evangelization of the Gospel. However, when he went to China, he eventually found out that people did not respect itinerant preachers but rather scholars. Since he was schooled in philosophy and theology, he also studied mathematics, cosmology, and astronomy under the direction of Christopher Clavius, the famed head of mathematicians at the Collegio Romano and astronomer who was a member of the Vatican Commission. Therefore, he changed out of his priestly Western robes in exchange for being seen as a Chinese scholar.

By the time he met the Chinese Emperor, he had lived in China since 1582 and gained fame for his knowledge of Chinese classics and his competency in astronomy, which helped him forecast solar eclipses. In ancient China, a solar eclipse can be a bad omen foretelling the end of a dynasty.

Matteo Ricci's willingness to lose himself in and immerse himself in Chinese culture and competently harness his knowledge helped change relations between the West and China for a while. But it was not meant to be, as subsequent encounters between the West and China became confrontational, even today. One can only wonder if Matteo had continued his work, what would it have done for the relationship between the West and China?

"Once I thought learning was a multifold experience and I would not refuse to travel [even] ten thousand Li to be able to question wise men and visit celebrated countries. But how long is a man's life? It is certain that many years are needed to acquire a complete science, based on a vast number of observations: and that's where one becomes old without the time to make use of this science. Is this not a painful thing?

And this is why I put great store by [geographical] maps and history: history for fixing [these observations], and maps for handing them on [to future generations].

Respectfully written by the European Matteo Ricci,
17 August 1602.

Written on the map of 坤舆万国全图, *Map of the Ten Thousand Countries of the Earth.*

Intuition Matters to Lead Change

"Can you show me any existing examples where this has worked?" A company board member asked my colleague, who had presented a creative approach for the business model after a comprehensive assessment of their limitations and seeing new possibilities.

My colleague left the meeting fuming.

"They asked us for innovation, and when we brought it to them, they f*cking asked us to benchmark. What the hell!" I told him to calm down and said that this is to be expected in our line of work. The fear of change lurks everywhere.

Change is hard to quantify, justify, and, worse, duplicate. Every situation is unique, even in the same industry, because the teams you work with differ from one another.

When Soviet Communism was in its death throes, communists in Moscow thought they could appeal to the Baltic States to remain communist and stay with the union, but it turns out it was the same communists who were leading the calls for democracy and an end to communism.

There is no carbon copy for change since it is yours to make. No amount of feasibility study can justify it. You have to see it in your heart, mind, and hands before you bring others in.

Many studies have been done on why entrepreneurs take risks. Results reveal that it is not logical and money is not the primary motivation.

"...there is the will to conquer: the impulse to fight, to prove oneself superior to others, to succeed for the sake, not of the fruits of success, but of success itself. From this aspect, economic action becomes akin to sport - there are financial races, or rather boxing-matches. The financial result is a secondary consideration."

- Joseph Schumpeter Austrian Economist

Taking risks is irrational and largely intuitive, which is why entrepreneurs pursue it. This is important because entrepreneurs win big by challenging the status quo.

The once-in-a-generation artist, songwriter, and entrepreneur Taylor Swift is proof of this. Starting in country music, she managed to intuitively pivot to other genres, such as pop and indie folk. Her music consisted of switching genres throughout her two decades in the music industry, with the most dramatic being switching from country to pop through her album, 1989. This move could be suicidal for a rising artist but she was not afraid to take risks and her loyal fans came along with her.

Certainly, it has not been a smooth journey. In a public dispute with her previous record company, Big Machine, which sold the master rights to her recordings, she retaliated by re-recording all her albums, thereby gaining personal control. What she has done is game-changing by breaking the stranglehold of record companies. She is now both a writer and a record company in full control of her intellectual property.

How powerful is Taylor Swift? There is literally a term called Swiftonomics, defined as the economic influence of musician Taylor Swift. Her recent decision to hold concerts only in Singapore for her Eras Tour nearly caused a diplomatic crisis in Southeast Asia.

Taylor Swift reached her position by trusting her intuition to challenge the status quo and win big—this is how she became a newly minted billionaire, Grammy Award winner, and a dominant cultural, political, and economic force.

Truly, Taylor Swift is the leading Changemaker in music for our age.

Dissolving to Gain New Wings

Steve Jobs's return to Apple was greeted with cult-like enthusiasm on stage at Macworld Boston. Using all that goodwill, he introduced the live satellite link with Bill Gates, widely considered as his nemesis. In one stroke, the hall exploded into loud jeers and boos.

It was a difficult moment but Steve knew he needed this reconciliation with Bill to put an end to the fight between PCs and Macs because he could see that a new battle was slowly emerging: the internet.

For those familiar with the famous 1984 Apple ad, in which a woman in a white top with a colorful Apple logo threw a hammer at a large screen of a man in gray speaking in an Orwellian tone, Bill's presence on a big screen with Steve appearing small and standing nearby became hard to watch for many Apple fans.

Not only did Steve want fans to accept working with Microsoft, but Bill had also acquired a part of Apple, too, through his investment of $150 million. For some, it was too much to swallow.

But after Steve got this over with and worked with Microsoft, he had the funding and the ability to focus on what truly mattered—leading Apple headlong into the internet age, which then set off the "i" era. The iPod, the iPhone, and then the iPad paved the way for Apple's eventual domination in the post-PC era. These moves would not have been possible had Apple continued to fight against Microsoft. Apple would ultimately exceed Microsoft's market value while Steve was alive.

Imagine being wrongly imprisoned for a long time, what do you think would happen to your mind? Now think 27 years—that is enough for a child to grow into adulthood. Yet when Nelson Mandela was freed by President F. W. de Klerk in 1990, he did not waste any time to settle old scores. No. Instead, he worked double-quick time in partnership with President Klerk to end apartheid in South Africa, for which they were both awarded the Nobel Peace Prize.

Nelson Mandela understood deeply that in order to truly turn the page, he had to lead by example. He remained a symbol of freedom while he was in prison. Now out of prison, he knew that he needed to be the symbol of peace. To realize this, he worked hard for reconciliation between racial groups.

He worked to heal deep wounds through the Truth and Reconciliation Commission to investigate human rights abuses. When he led the government, he had a broad coalition which updated the constitution.

Both Steve Jobs and Nelson Mandela understood that unless they could let go of past rivalries or issues, they would not find new wings to fly.

No Flight Without Falling

We all worry about failing—I do, too. But failing is a teaching moment, and many times, it is important to fail early to know where we must go. When we were kids, the fall moments were the best moments to help us perfect our walking and growing.

With colleagues and partners at the Paul H. O'Neill School of Public and Environmental Affairs Executive Education department, we have been teaching a leadership formation course, Holistic Leadership, since 2021. It is an eight-part series that is like a personal discernment and examination to know our being, the moments we are in, and how to act in alignment with our values to lead others.

It has been an extraordinary experience where we facilitate mid to senior-level leaders who come from the Americas, Africa, Asia, and Europe through 7-8 sessions of leadership formation. Participants come from various industries such as medical institutions, non-profit organizations, and even small family businesses.

What I treasured most during these sessions are the many personal encounters I shared with people from around the world. In this course, we also have a specific segment where leaders have to discern the moment when they have to take that leap of faith.

There was one leader who shared that she was aiming for the apex leadership role in their organization because she had dedicated so much time building it. She felt ready and she believed she was the best candidate to serve. But before this course, she would not have the audacity to aim for it.

She advocated for herself yet through a somewhat unclear and painful process, she did not get the job. However, in an email to share with us this experience, she said:

"Ironically, the immediate thought I had when the consultant told me I wouldn't be moving on through the interview process was one of relief: 'well, that just made my decision easier.' It didn't really - I'm still struggling with what I want to do next, where I want to go, if I even want to go. But the relief has stayed - all of a sudden, I have all of this time and energy back - because I'm not trying so hard to prove myself worthy for this job that I thought I wanted so much. I did want it, and I did dedicate time, and I am going to be feeling the loss of that - but every so often, I also feel

this inflated sense of hope and excitement - like, now I can do ANYTHING."

- Kate

Don't you feel the same way sometimes?

In the early days of Consulus, I was so worried about failing that I felt we could not survive alone. So, from 2007 to 2009, we joined an international design firm from Australia led by someone I admire greatly, Ken Cato, one of the best designers in the world. He has worked on almost all the major brands in Australia, such as Qantas. So, at that point in our history, we were known as Consulus Cato Partners.

Though I admired Ken, our views on growing a global design practice diverged. He is a big believer in design as a craft for the mind, whereas I am a big believer that design is an instrument to change the world.

In one eventful conversation, Ken said to me, "We are designers, Lawrence. Just focus on design." Then I replied, "Ken, I believe in another path in which design can direct strategy."

Mind you, at that time, I was a much younger man speaking with one of the best designers in the world. But I felt the courage within me to claim that space. We eventually split ways in 2009 and found our own way, and that was how Consulus truly took off by creating its own methods for creative change.

Free Yourself to Explore the Boundless Skies

To get your astronaut wings, your spacecraft must at least reach the Karman line or the official line between the Earth's atmosphere and the space situated about 330,000 feet above mean sea level. It is still within the thermosphere of the Earth but way above the typical reach of conventional aircrafts that fly between 31,000 to 42,000 feet.

When you look up into the sky, that is how high you can go if you choose to. Imagine what a caterpillar feels, looking up into the sky and seeing how butterflies fly freely.

Is the ability to achieve something seemingly impossible a matter of competence? Or is it about conquering the mind to attain competence?

From what I have learned and experienced, it is always the latter. Sadly, to most people, if you tell them that any pivot is possible, many will dismiss you outright, which is why I say change is hard.

People also assume it is hard in their minds first.

The Wright brothers did not think so when they attempted the first flight.

Jerrie Mock certainly did not share this belief either, otherwise she would not have become the first woman to fly solo around the world in 1964.

The greatest enemy of any pivot is the fear in your mind and fighting it matters. The quote from the second Dune movie by Director Denis Villeneuve exemplifies this so aptly:

"I must not fear.

Fear is the mind-killer.

Fear is the little-death that brings total obliteration.

I will face my fear.

I will permit it to pass over me and through me.

And when it has gone past, I will turn the inner eye to see its path.

Where the fear has gone there will be nothing. Only I will remain."

So, the idea of a competent pivot is to free your mind from fear and then facing the challenges in a methodical way, one step at a time.

Elon Musk managed to launch a rocket that goes far beyond the Karman line simply because he was self-motivated. He engineered it all the way with his team, starting with facing his fears and because he kept faith, he kept persevering despite massive setbacks.

Obama did not become the first black president of the United States by simply shouting "Yes we can!" He attracted an A-team to help him build one of the most insightful and inclusive ground operations to shape a movement that changed history.

All of the persons above had one thing in common: they conquered their fears by taking a staircase approach, by breaking things into manageable steps thus competently building their capability to cross their own Karman lines.

So the question is: what do you see in your mind, limits to be afraid of or a Karman line to be crossed?

Changemaking Through Competent Pivot

Like a caterpillar that transforms into a butterfly, the process of being and doing is all about taking the right steps to prepare yourself, your mind, heart, and hands for change. To evaluate if you are ready and prepared to go on that journey to pivot, consider the following:

Acknowledging that the pivot is now
i. It is possible to get a grip on fleeting change
ii. How are you pivoting from crawl to flight?
iii. What do you need to lose to find new pivots?

Mindspace for pivot
iv. Do you trust your intuition to lead change?
v. What must dissolve for new wings to emerge?

Pivotal leap into the future

vi. Will you know where to fall to fly?

vii. Is the sky the limit for you?

Pivoting is a constant process for one's self and the organizations we seek to shape as Changemakers. More importantly, it asks how we can be faithful to our cause and creative vision to impact the world anew. However, to do that, we need to observe and see the turns in the universe.

We cannot predict the future, but we can see signs. Seeing beyond is what we will focus on next.

"观今夜之天象，而知天下之大事。"
"By observing the celestial
phenomena tonight, one can discern
the great events of the world."

Zhuge Liang,
a Chinese statesman, strategist, and inventor

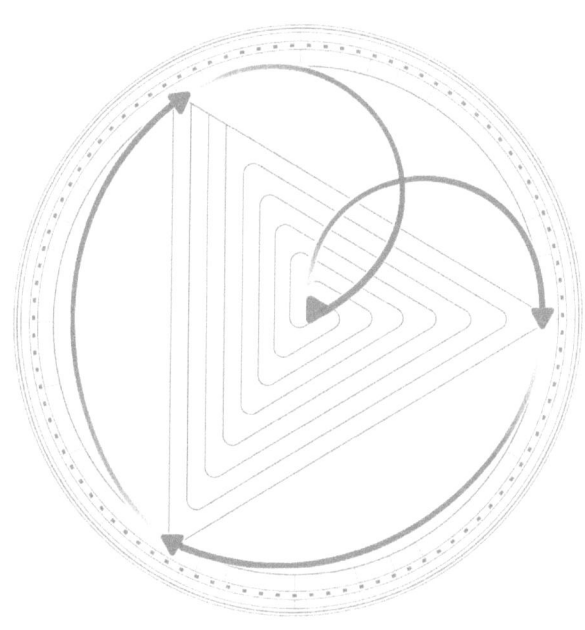

THREAD 61

Seeing Beyond

Emperor Huang knows that unless there is foresight and wisdom to see beyond, his vast empire will continue to be insecure. And now in a time of crisis with the threat of war looming from the North, the Emperor is in need of someone of such caliber.

Even the Emperor knows he must be humble enough to seek counsel. Emperor Huang is now near the summit of Huangshan (Yellow Mountain), where the famous green tea, also known as Huangshan Yunwu, is produced. He could see why great tea was grown here because the area feels like heaven, with an ethereal beauty characterized by jagged granite peaks, twisted pine trees, and swirling mists.

Ming Yue, in hurried steps, rushed forward as fast as she could, even though she had advanced in age. She was still fit since she had led armies to war before for the Emperor's father.

"Your Majesty, I am so sorry I did not receive news of your coming," she said.

Emperor Huang replied, "I have sent for you a few times, but you have said your time is over and refused to come, so now the monk has to come and retrieve the scriptures (和尚出山, 拿经去).

"I am so sorry for my insolence, I am at your service," Ming Yue replied.

"Let us walk and bring us some of the fine tea of these mountains," the Emperor commanded.

"You served my father well and achieved many victories. Now, the North threatens us again, but this time, it is different. It is fiercer and quicker than the last time. We have lost a few border cities to them, and they are getting closer. I have brave warriors, but I lack something else: foresight and strategy. Ming Yue, what must I do?"

Ming Yue, after hearing the Emperor's sigh and concerns, then requested an audience beneath the night sky. As both stood under the canopy of stars, Ming Yue began narrating a parable.

"In the days of old, a mighty oak stood tall and strong in the midst of a vast forest. Its branches reached for the heavens, but its roots delved deep into the earth. Yet, despite its strength, the oak knew the importance of flexibility in the face of adversity. One year, a fierce storm descended upon the forest with howling winds and torrential rain. The oak, rooted firmly in the ground, stood its ground against the

tempest. But a wise old willow, bending gracefully with the wind, survived unscathed."

"Your Majesty," Ming Yue continued, "just as the willow adapts to the changing winds, so too must we adapt our strategies to the ever-shifting tides of war. Like the stars guiding us in the night sky, we must align our actions with the rhythms of nature and the movements of our adversaries."

At this moment, the pavilion was filled with the aroma of green tea. As the servants served Emperor Huang, he understood the wisdom hidden within its simplicity. He understood he had to order his generals to study the terrain, observe the heavens, and wait for the opportune moment to strike.

The Emperor asked Ming Yue to return to the palace to help him plan his next moves. As the seasons turned and stars wheeled overhead, Ming Yue guided the Emperor's forces with precision and foresight. When the time was right, they launched a counteroffensive that harnessed their indigenous knowledge of the terrain and the season, safeguarding the realm from danger.

Even today, the legend of Ming Yue, the Sage of the stars and nature, to which even the Emperor had to come to seek advice, lives on in the annals of history.

Essence of Seeing Beyond

"There is no better teacher than history in determining the future... There are answers worth billions of dollars in $30 history book."

- Charlie Munger,
American businessman, investor, and philanthropist.

Somewhere on Wall Street, just before the tectonic financial crash of 2008, Hollywood recreated a scene from the movie The Big Shot.

A banker from Deutsche Bank wanted to pitch to a group of investors to short the housing market. It is worth noting that at that time, the housing market was thought to be an impregnable fortress, a safe bet.

As the investors entered the presentation, they saw a Jenga set built up before them.

On the side of these stacked wooden blocks, the ratings of the tiers AAA, AA, BBB, BB, and B were written. The banker went on to explain:

"This is a basic mortgage bond. The original ones were simple, thousands of AAA mortgages bundled together and sold with a guarantee from the US government. But the modern day ones are private and are made up of layers of tranches, with the AAA highest rated getting paid first and the lowest, B rated getting paid last and taking on defaults first.

Obviously if you're buying B levels you can get paid more. Hey, they're risky, so sometimes they fail...

But somewhere along the line these B and BB level tranches went from risky to dog shit. I'm talking rock bottom FICO scores, no income verification, adjustable rates... Dog shit.

Default rates are already up from 1 to 4 percent. If they rise to 8 percent, and they will, a lot of these BBB's are going to zero."

We will never know if the scene did happen, but with all that we know now, the crash of 2008 was a long time coming. Considered as one of the top five financial earthquakes of the world, it led to the loss of millions of homes and jobs, depleted US$ 2 trillion from the global economy, and required the world's governments to guarantee the value of their banks to prevent pandemonium.

You may not be a fortune teller but it is hard for people to lie about time, money, and relationships. Seeing how much people spend their time versus what they say they would and witnessing where they put actual money in despite risks or gain, are reliable tell-tale signs of true intent.

Seeing who their friends and enemies are, these are also truth tellers and indicative of their next steps.

Charlie Munger and Warren Buffett made money far away from the distractions of Wall Street by being in Omaha to build Berkshire Hathaway, a globally renowned investment firm. In its storied run of 58 years, the stock has appreciated at a 19.8% compound annual growth rate, compared to the 9.9% annualized return for the S&P 500. The duo made their long-term bets, taking a surgical view on time, money, and relationships as truth tellers.

We should learn from them.

This is what seeing beyond means. It is about focusing on the essential truths objectively and not being swayed by emotions and spectacles.

Walls and Watch Towers Do Not Secure Empires

The capital city of Bangladesh, Dhaka, means "watchtower," this is according to the Rajatarangini, a historical account written by a Kashmiri Brahman

Dhaka has been one of the oldest continuously inhabited mega cities since the 7th century which has been ruled by various empires, from the Hindu, Buddhist, and Mughal to the European empires. It bore witness to its own rise, decline, and rebirth as it evolved from the ancient world to modern times.

With the strained traffic of meandering cars and the cacophony of horns along Kazi Nazrul Islam Avenue, you can certainly feel how this historic city struggles to keep up with modernity. Once one of the wealthiest citadels in the world, the town was a crown jewel in a region that generated 12% of the world's GDP during the Mughal period.

In present times, however, Dhaka struggles with poverty and in providing opportunities for millions of young people.

In search of a better future, many choose to go overseas to work in fields outside their expertise or skill set. For example, a graduate in business may choose to work as a construction worker in harsh conditions in Dubai.

Yet, Bangladesh has started to thrive again as one of the fastest growing economies in the world. The growing number of BMWs and Mercedes in the middle of its infamous traffic jams is a sign of it. However, economic growth still needs to be improved for the vast majority of this nation which has a population of about 150 million.

While the traffic was coming to a standstill, I found myself caught in the midst of Dhaka's bustling streets. My heart was racing because I had changed the entire slide deck of my talk last night after a pivotal conversation with young Bangladeshi friends but more on that soon.

This was in 2012, I am in Dhaka at the invitation of Professor Philip Kotler, recognized as the "Father of Modern Marketing." He has called for a gathering of about 50 experts in marketing, creatives, and other Changemakers for his inaugural World Marketing Summit.

Professor Kotler is an untiring champion of change, and this event had an audacious goal; he declared it as a summit that hopes to ignite positive change. Prime Minister Sheikh Hasina kicked off the two-and-a-half-day summit attended by 3,000 persons, with many youths in attendance.

Each speaker was assigned a youth leader who assisted us if we needed help. My young guide and friend who helped me tremendously is Mohammad Imtiaz Hossain, an earnest 23-year-old studying business and marketing who spoke good English. The first day of the summit went well, with many speakers talking about how marketing is changing towards impact, what one needs to do to find success, the new trends of marketing, and so on.

But during the day, I chatted with Imtiaz to understand Bangladesh and to know his views about the future of the country. He shared about the political challenges, the economic struggles, and how he sees limited opportunities for himself, even as he and his friends continue to study hard.

In the evening, Imtiaz brought another friend to meet me. I asked the same question and was met with the same sense of uncertainty and pessimism. The common question that both Imtiaz and his friend asked me was about Singapore since they had heard so much about it. "How did Singapore change to become so successful?" I remember them asking.

After a while, I asked Imtiaz and his friend about Bangladesh. I thought: with its great culture and history, surely, the country should be able to do better than Singapore. Imtiaz then looked at me and asked, "Is change possible?"

After that heart-breaking question from Imtiaz and his friend which stumped me, I decided to change my entire deck towards something that can be relevant for the youth.

I wanted my talk to be like a gift for them, to market how change is possible for them, to inspire them that if tiny Singapore can do it despite all odds, then they, too, could do it.

I felt responsible as one of the youngest speakers invited in the event, so I did my presentation with all my heart. One of my fellow speakers, Craig, wrote this in his blog about my talk:

> *"Lawrence Chong moved the energy level of the group to a high level with his presentation. He called on participants to have a purpose - 'how will you shape the world?' And always ask yourself 'What does it mean? Why am I doing this?' He stated that the 1% who shape the world think deeply about meaning, are restless to change the status quo, and have a strong sense of obligation to their industry, their country or the world that supersedes everything else in their lives. Judging from the ovations and cheering by the end of his talk, there were a lot of students who want to be among those 1%ers."*

From the experience, I understood this hard truth: a wealthy and successful city will only be successful for a while. To sustain that success, the next generations must find the courage and confidence to build on the success of their predecessors because once that confidence is lost, it is hard to recover, even with a rich legacy.

The Humble Monk Who Came to Retrieve Scriptures

Deng Xiaoping is a small-sized man who lived a large life. Before he became known as the 'paramount leader,' which is the imperial equivalent of the supreme power of China in the 20th century, he faced death and was once ostracized by the communist party. For someone who was supposed to know everything, acknowledging that he could learn from one of the smallest countries in the world was quite something.

Deng visited Singapore from November 12 to 14, 1978. The last time he came to the sunny island was when he was 16 years old, in 1920, while on his way from China to France on a work and study program. Fifty-eight years since then, he could see the rapid transformation of Singapore from a British colony to a thriving modern city-state. Other than China, Singapore is a unique independent nation in the middle of Southeast Asia where ethnic Chinese form the majority.

During Deng's only trip to Singapore, Lee Kuan Yew remarked that if Singapore, with a population of three-quarters Chinese, many of whom were descendants of coolies, could achieve a certain level of development, how much more could China, with its long history and vast talent?

Deng, a person who kept his cards close to his heart, would take heed of this suggestion. On an essential trip to the south of China to drum up support for his economic reforms, he said:

"China should learn from Singapore because society in Singapore is quite orderly. They managed things very strictly. We ought to use their experience as a model. And we ought to manage things even better than they do."

Since the 80s till now, hundreds of delegations from China have visited Singapore, including almost every important leader in China. They studied every detail of Singapore's development—from housing, communication, politics, etc.

Singapore remains the only country to have significant joint industrial development projects with China, such as the Tianjin Eco-city project focusing on sustainable urban planning and development.

Throughout Deng's leadership and reform of the Chinese economy, despite the setbacks, the country grew from strength to strength with its GDP having risen tenfold.

According to the World Bank in 2022, the number of people in China with incomes below the International Poverty Line amounting to $1.90 per day had fallen by close to 800 million over the past 40 years.

The economic reforms that Deng implemented in the 1980s had a lasting effect. In fact, globally, China's share of extreme poverty reduction is close to three-quarters. One of the reasons for this is his willingness to learn from a smaller entity.

Seeing Why it is Fiercer and Quicker than the Last Time

The train moved quietly despite traveling at a high speed of about 120-240 miles per hour. This is China's high-speed rail, and I am on my way to Huizhou with my business partner Mingxi from the border of Hong Kong. This is 2024, and China now has the world's longest and most extensively used rail system with a total length of 27,961.70 miles.

Compared to the US, which just broke ground for the first high-speed rail in the country on 27 April 2024, China is light years ahead.

Wes Edens, a billionaire businessman, invested on Brightline West, the $12 billion Las Vegas-to-SoCal railway, which will be supported by billions from the Biden Administration.

The US does not lack competence and the funds, but in comparison to China, why did it take so long?

Americans have long complained about Amtrak, the national passenger railroad company of the United States. The problem has long existed. But where is the solution?

Before the United States became the world's superpower, it was the first to embark on a pivotal project to connect the continental USA. Aided by federal grants, there was a massive spike in railroad construction after the Civil War. Trackage jumped from 35,000 miles in 1865 to 254,000 miles in 1916, the eve of America's foray into World War I

By the time World War II ended, the US had moved away from developing railways to developing the interstate highway system in 1956, which became a network of 47,000 roads to ease busy and crumbling roads.

What does this tell you? It tells you that whatever you seed today, you will harvest tomorrow. But first, you have to see beyond. The railway and interstate plans were visionary which is the same with China's vision for high-speed rail. These are projects with decades-long impact.

But this also tells you that in everything you see, there is a need to act on it. You might not know how the world will turn, but it is better to see ahead to remain in the flow because it will for sure be fiercer and quicker than the last time.

Jensen Huang, the founder of Nvidia, shared at the 2024 SIEPR Economic Summit at Stanford University that since his company has been working hard to build the infrastructure for artificial intelligence for decades, he believes that the cost of computing is approaching zero. This has opened the floodgates for AI innovation which was the result of a million-fold improvement gain from deep learning costs in the last ten years.

So, with this new fast-moving AI infrastructure in place, there will be a million-fold increase in computational capabilities in the next decade. He foresees a shift from static learning models to constantly evolving dynamic processes. I believe soon, even your website can speak with you, give you a rundown on the transactions that happened, or even redesign itself to be more effective.

As of May 2024, Nvidia has a market cap of US$ 2.57 trillion. This makes Nvidia the world's third most valuable company by market cap and one that is certainly in the fast flow of the future.

The idea is: a decade of seeding for another decade of growth. Anything big and pivotal requires a decade of effort for a decade of exponential growth.

Which decade is yours?

The Intransigent Oak Tree With Deep Roots

Whether you love him or hate him, and there are plenty in both camps, Elon Musk is the singular person of our times.

If Steve Jobs is considered the creative genius of an earlier age, Elon is our creative disruptor who has made a name for himself from the automobile to the space industry, which are heavily regulated sectors with deeply entrenched players who have done things in a particular way for decades.

You have the likes of Toyota, in the car industry, which has dominated mass manufacturing of cars, and then you have Boeing and Lockheed, which have both been part of the aviation and space industry for many years. Both industries are multi-billion businesses which made money by setting the rules and the entire supply chain to enable the industry.

The issue with these companies, however, is that the more entrenched they are in the industry, the more expensive it is to enact change. This is also why the barrier to entry is high for new entrants.

So, for Elon, who has not only challenged both sectors but has also become one of the leading players in both, to succeed in one industry is a feat. But to succeed in both? That is sui generis.

However, the main reason why he was able to succeed was simply that neither industry expected him to be able to sustain himself and succeed. They did not change fast enough to meet the challenge of the disruptor. It was his unwavering determination and resilience that allowed him to overcome these odds.

To challenge the existing players, Elon put all his wealth on the line and worked very hard to lower costs and achieve speed. It was a systematic method that has come to be known as Elon Musk's Algorithm which involves the following:

- **Question every requirement**
- **Delete any part of the process you can**
- **Simplify and optimise**
- **Accelerate cycle time**
- **Automate**

These steps proved so formidable that even Toyota engineers, alarmed by the growing speed and scale of their competitor's ability to produce cars at scale, took apart a Tesla to understand how he and his team did it since they were impressed that it was a new way of making a car.

Much of Elon's thinking on reusability and on the 'fail early' approach has been adopted for the growing space industry.

Elon's approaches have forced a complete rethink of the manufacturing and development processes of the space and automobile industries that for sure will never be the same again. In a way, the intransigent oak trees in both sectors have been upended.

The Wise Willow That Adapts to the Changing Winds

When do you assess the changing winds in order to improve?

Typically, a non-profit or a company will do annual strategic retreats for just a few days, but how far would it go?

At a personal level, we might take sabbaticals to see our future anew before adjusting our posture.

The question is whether we dare to consider deeply and adapt systematically when we sense the winds are changing.

Angelo Giuseppe Roncalli was a lifelong diplomat of the Vatican who had a distinguished career serving France, Bulgaria, Greece, and Turkey. During the Second World War, while serving in Turkey, and by then he was already an archbishop, he helped save the lives of many Jews fleeing the holocaust by providing them with transit visas and paperwork to leave Europe.

But on 28 October 1958, in a conclave to elect a new Pope, he was surprisingly elected, taking on the new title Pope John XXIII. At 76 years old, many expected him to be a caretaker leader of the Catholic Church as it took 11 ballots to decide on one candidate.

So, you can just imagine the surprise of the Cardinals who did not expect this Pope to do much. But as he sensed how much the world had changed after the Second World War, the Church seems stuck in a time vault. Because of intuition, Pope John XXIII called for the Second Vatican Council. In the history of this 2000-year-old institution, 20 church councils have been held to clarify church teachings and meet the changes in human history, so this would be the 21st. By this time, there were 530 million Catholics worldwide

The Second Vatican Council, which lasted from 1962 to 1965, involved 2500 bishops from every continent. During this time, there was a review of every aspect of the Church, from its relations with the modern world and with other religions to how to better equip itself with the challenges of a secular world. The council also simplified worship to make it more accessible—this included changing the use of Latin in its services, which was considered by many as hard to understand.

The reforms unleashed a social revolution within the church and focused more on changing mindsets and promoting inclusivity in terms of identity and driving social change. Pope John XXIII did not live to see the completion of the council he called since he died of stomach cancer before it concluded. But the reforms he set in motion prepared the Catholic Church to counter its most formidable nemesis at the time, communism.

Stalin infamously questioned the number of tanks the Pope had. It was a dismissive remark as he questioned the Pope's relevance and power to mobilize the people.

Traditionally, Popes have either been Italian or French, but the reforms that Pope John XXIII implemented have opened so many doors that on 16 October 1978, the conclave elected the first ever Slavic Pope from Poland. Pope John Paul II became the first pope from Eastern Europe which was part of the Soviet Union during the Cold War.

Communism is an atheist system, and so when Pope John Paul II expressed his plan to visit his homeland of Poland and gather millions of Polish people to pray, hope began to flourish. The belief that faith can overcome the dictatorship of communism prevailed among the people.

When the Pope later endorsed the non-violent labor movement of Solidarność in Poland, it eventually created conditions and calls for peaceful demonstrations that ultimately resulted in the fall of communism and the rise of democracy.

Truly, the intuition of Pope John XXIII shows that wise willows do stand the test of time.

Align our Actions with the Rhythms of Nature

In an interview with Charlie Rose, the renowned host who has interviewed titans and presidents, Bill Gates shared what he learned from Warren Buffett about time. It is an illuminating exchange about mastery of time:

(In the Studio of Charlie Rose)

Bill Gates: I also remember Warren showing me his calendar.

Charlie Rose: Oh, I love this. (Looking through the small calendar journal of warren Buffett)

Bill Gates: You know, I had every minute packed and I thought that was the only way you could do things. And the fact that he is so careful about -- he has days.

Charlie Rose: That there's nothing on it.

Bill Gates: That's there's nothing on it.

Warren Buffett: Absolutely. (LAUGHTER)

Bill Gates: It's very high tech, be careful, you might not understand it.

Charlie Rose: This is the week of April, of which there are only three entries for a week.

Warren Buffett: There will be four maybe by April. (LAUGHTER)

Bill Gates: File taxes.

Charlie Rose: So it taught you what, not to crowd yourself too much and give yourself time to read and think and...

Bill Gates: Right. You control your time. And that sitting and thinking may be a much higher priority than a normal CEO, where's there all these demands and you feel like you need to go and see all these people. It's not a proxy of your seriousness that you fill every minute in your schedule.

Warren Buffett: And people will want your time. I mean, it's the only thing you can't buy. I mean, I can buy anything I want, basically, but I can't buy time.

Charlie Rose: And so to have time is the most precious thing you can have.

Warren Buffett: I better be careful with it. There is no way I will be able to buy more time.

Charlie Rose: And living in Omaha makes that easier?

Warren Buffett: That makes it a lot easier. For 54 years, I spent five minutes going each way. Now, just imagine that was half an hour each way, I would know the words to a lot more songs, and that's about it.

Charlie Rose: It adds up, doesn't it?

Warren Buffett: It really adds up. If you're talking an hour a day difference coming and going, and that's two and a half percent of the person's work week, that means 40 years, you're talking about a year.

Here are two of the wealthiest persons in the world who created wealth on their own by changing their respective fields. Warren Buffett's thinking on investment and finance is a principle on his own. Then you have Bill Gates, who built one of the world's largest software companies and is now disrupting philanthropy in a scientific and impactful way.

Having said this, not everyone can have the luxury of taking time. How people spend their time is very different from one another. But then again, the key to this thread is not to carbon copy but to examine.

I believe it is important to have an idea of how you want to master your own time, resources, and relationships based on your unique situation. It is about having intentionality in what you want and to reflect by yourself on what truly matters in your life. Here, we should be more focused on change-making and having an impact.

I have developed a method that was introduced in PersonalCORE, which I call the **The Three Mastery of Time, Networks, and Resources Approach**.

In this framework, you need to commit to spending the right amount of time, building the right networks, and gathering resources to eventually create a masterpiece of impact with the help of others.

Mastery of Time: Examine how you will devote weekly or monthly to improving your capabilities and impact.

Mastery of Networks: Evaluate the networks or communities you are involved in. Are you deepening relationships to be in a position of influence for a positive impact?

Mastery of Resources: Assess how you can accumulate the right experiences, partners, and resources that you can harness in the future.

Changemaking by Seeing Beyond

Nothing happens by chance. Climate change is the consequence of human action. We cannot predict the future, but
we can prepare for all kinds of scenarios.

This entire section has been dedicated to ponder the
improbable:

See beyond existential limits

i.   **All empires have a shelf life.**

ii. **Are you humble to learn from an unlikely source?**

See beyond what has changed

iii. **There is a reason for the speed of today.**

iv. **Who are the intransigent oak trees?**

See beyond to adapt

v.   Are you wise and adaptable?

vi. How to gain mastery over self to achieve change?

Seeing beyond calls for regular practice. It is important to be mindful of strategic pauses to reflect on your current state and how you are spending time to achieve impact.

This phase is going to be critical as it is increasingly going to be an uncertain and untethered world. To discern our next steps, we must be open to probabilities and improbabilities.

Working with organizations around the world—from enterprises, global foundations, governments, to even an entire city—has given my team and I unique foresight on how the world might change.

The next set of threads discusses eight trends, some positive, and others deeply worrying, based on time, the type of relationships emerging, and the amount of resources being poured in. These are some of my observations for the future.

The Four Futures

During the height of the COVID-19 pandemic, when my team and I analyzed money and talent flows, we identified Four Futures of Change or FEDS — four areas that will have seismic shifts on the future of humanity and the economy. This does not mean, however, that other trends do not matter. But these are four foundational shifts that will impact humanity in many ways. In summary they are:

1. Food Generation and Consumption

How humanity produces and consumes food will seismically affect how much we will evolve and succeed as a multi-planetary species. This will also severely impact economies whenever agricultural methods evolve and as climate change affects this sphere. We will see the rise of new food systems and not look at it in the same way in another decade.

2. Environmental and Climate Change Economy

How humanity evolves in terms of innovation and regulation to address the climate crisis will change how we live, work, and play. Fighting the rising heat will affect urbanization and force governments to take drastic action to dramatically rethink the cost and design of public infrastructure. The era of "green washing" will quickly give way to pragmatic solutions to urgent climate change issues.

3. Data that can think for humanity

How humanity reacts to different kinds of data that can generate various results and recommendations will rewire our minds and thinking. New tools have always shaped human behavior, but artificial intelligence (AI)—the kind that can imagine futures for humanity—will either be limiting or liberating. The current hold of social media echo chambers also means that there is a danger of utilizing AI to limit what humanity can or should think.

4. Space for humans

How humanity will handle living and exploring planets will expand human consciousness. With so many players in this space, it is no longer probable but inevitable. In a decade or so, space mining will be a regular feature. With the number of successful launches into outer space becoming the norm, a flight to the moon in two decades could be considered a walk in the park.

Let us review these areas one at a time.

FOOD –
How You Plant and Eat Changes the World

As the majestic sun rose over the outskirts of Abuja, I walked the sprawling grounds of the beautiful SCL farm with my partner, Dr. Andrew Kwasari, while learning about all the different regenerative agriculture techniques.

At one point, we talked about an approach that his impact enterprise uses to teach Nigerian farmers how to regenerate lands that have lost their topsoil without using harmful fertilizers.

Before the rainy season, you have to dig a pit in the shape of a half-moon and keep the rest of what you have dug up in a crescent shape so that when the rain comes, it flows into this pit and stays there. In the middle of the pit, you have to put in dead leaves or what you call biomass. This then acts as a sponge when the rain comes and retains the water. This whole process can generate rich compost and act as a fertilizer for new plants. This technique, also known as 'half moon,' is based on African wisdom and practice that many have forgotten.

As we walked the beautiful grounds, we saw many half-moons filled with various trees and vegetables.

Discovering agriculture changed humanity and helped raise our level of intelligence as humans gained a good staple diet. Twelve thousand years ago, agriculture, or what we understand now as the "Neolithic Revolution," allowed the rise of towns that turned into cities and shaped the idea of civilization. From the Egyptians to the Chinese, the idea of being able to grow food to overcome famine has meant the rise and fall of empires.

Today is no different.

Food shortages have caused revolutions throughout human history, and the rise in food prices in 2010 was an important trigger for the Arab Spring. Food is undoubtedly big business. In fact, revenue in the food industry in 2024 is about US$ 9 trillion. The largest segment is meat, which is about US$ 1.46 trillion.

With a world population of 8 billion people, there is a lot to feed. Yet ongoing wars and disruption to supply chains have continued to plague this sector. As a trillion-dollar sector, it matters a lot to understand change in the food sector.

The growing scale of current hunger, either due to war or climate change, is staggering. Based on available data, more than 333 million people face acute levels of food shortage, as in they do not know where to get their next meal.

More importantly, new innovation is entering this space to disrupt the market. Alternative proteins received almost US$ 16 billion worth of investments. This is not an easy sector, as I have observed being involved in some venture-funded projects on my own. It requires scale, a supply chain, and new regulations to allow humans to consume food safely.

Furthermore, a bigger sum of money is going into agri-food technology. According to the AgriFoodTech Investment Report in 2022, the AgriFoodTech category received US$ 51.7 billion. This shows the potential of experiencing a faster gain in impact versus using alternative protein as the latter will need to cross a lot of regulatory hurdles and would be more costly. Moreover, in many countries, food production is still not as efficient regarding land use and yield. Another interesting development is that many experiments have been conducted on growing leafy greens in space to aid interplanetary travel. This gives us a new understanding of agriculture in zero-gravity conditions. As a kid, I was fascinated with the idea of space farms. What was once a wild idea, is now slowly becoming reality.

NASA developed the vegetable production system, or Veggie which was first implemented in the International Space Station on 7th May 2014 to test how food can be grown in space and how water can be delivered to plants, which is complicated in zero-gravity environments.

The growing food crisis, the rise of unusual alliances in the pursuit of food production, and the seismic shift in eating practices and talent will shape the current landscape and the future in new ways.

ENVIRONMENT –
How You Creatively Harness and
Scale Changes the Earth's Lifeline

At 48,050.4 mi², Sarawak, which is the same size as the Malaysian peninsula, holds some of the richest biodiverse lands in the world. But for a long time, the state's primary source of wealth is mining, felling of trees, and essentially extracting from nature.

However, now that the world is pouring money into sustainability, the state government of Sarawak is very astute to see that it is not just good for the economy but politics too as it allows the government to uplift the development of indigenous communities. Malaysia has experienced an upheaval in its political climate. Up until the publishing of this book, there have already been four prime ministers over 5 years. Against this backdrop, the state government of Sarawak is embarking on a massive master plan different from the past.

Instead of building more, it is now focusing on ways to preserve biodiversity and make money out of these efforts.

It is always an illuminating experience for me whenever I meet State Premier Tan Sri Abang Johari Tun Openg when he fluently talks about data regarding hydrogen and carbon credit. Premier's vision is to turn Sarawak into a sustainability powerhouse. At present, Sarawak is already powered 70% by hydropower.

What is happening in Sarawak is a litmus test for the world.

Saving the planet can no longer be about protests and stoppages of work. The massive COP28, with all its glitz and grandstanding, managed to only produce a weak statement that calls for a transition away from fossil fuels.

The only viable strategy to meet the power of fossil fuel firms is to replace the current carbon-based economy at scale through economic incentives. This takes the combined strength of capital, government, and entrepreneurship. This is easier said than done as many projects are capital-intensive and the projects that the Premier of Sarawak talks about will require talent and billions.

Moreover, not every country can commit their attention in enabling this to happen. President Biden had a hard time with his climate action plan for America, yet just in February 2024, oil and gas companies and environmental groups filed dueling legal challenges to the Biden administration's five-year plan to offer drilling leases in the Gulf of Mexico.

However, there is a growing convergence of singular scalable green projects, and mass financing is getting closer to changing the game.

Green tech investment is also rising exponentially. According to BloombergNEF, investment in low-carbon technologies reached US$ 755 billion in 2021 and is expected to reach a trillion dollars in the near future.

Last year, I went to see a tree I planted on a farm in Kuching, Sarawak, and within a year, it shot up to 3 meters high. We call it the FutureTrees project, and it is dedicated to land that has lost its topsoil. The species is known as Empress Trees or Revotropix Paulownia, which Bloomberg Magazine describes as one of the world's most reliable carbon capture trees. I am involved in this project because of my partner Dato Chris whose idea is to plant 10 million trees. This is just a tiny drop in the number of trees needed worldwide, but it is growing as a massive movement.

According to the United Nations Environmental Program, approximately 1.9 billion trees are planted annually. The report also reveals that close to 158 million trees around the planet are replanted every month.

The World Economic Forum's target, though, is 1 trillion trees by 2030, so in my view, planting trees at scale is important. But being able to finance that planting quickly and build an economy out of it is also paramount.

A research team headed by Bastin Jean-Francois of ETH-Zurich, Switzerland, created a model to estimate the planet's restoration potential by directly measuring the world's forest cover. They surmised that the planet could accommodate another 900 million hectares of forests (2.2 billion acres) which is about 25% more forest cover. If ½ trillion trees are planted, about 205 gigatons of carbon are captured (1 gigaton = 1 billion metric tons). This could reverse almost two decades of carbon emissions from human activities at the present rate. Hence, the ability to plant trees matters a lot in reversing carbon emissions.

What I saw in both Abuja and Kuching is this: when more trees take root, they bring vast benefits to the communities and the local economy.

With a realistic convergence of talent and financing, the focus on making sure our solutions are scalable is key instead of just focusing on sporadic projects.

DATA –
Feeding the Data Mothership to Rule Them All

"Once men turned their thinking over to machines in the hope that this would set them free. But that only permitted other men with machines to enslave them."

- Frank Herbert, Dune

On a chilly night at a Soviet Nuclear Early Warning System camp, alarms shrieked loudly with the word "LAUNCHED" etched in bright red.

Lieutenant Colonel Stanislav Petrov, who was not supposed to be on duty, was now staring at the screen, in which the computer was saying the United States had launched a few intercontinental ballistic missiles (ICBM) in the direction of the Soviet Union. Colonel Petrov stood in for the regular person on duty who was sick.

Colonel Petrov was an engineer and scientist whose day job was to take charge of the algorithm for signals coming from satellites and sensors. During this time, the Soviets' own early warning satellites were new and untested, and this was at the height of Cold War tensions, so it was a nerve-racking responsibility for him.

According to protocol, he is supposed to immediately alert his superiors of the Soviet Union so that they can lob back nuclear missiles. Both sides will die—that was supposed to be the game plan: mutual and assured destruction.

However, Petrov decided to make his own decision. He would not trust the computer. He deduced that if the US wanted to end the Soviet Union, then why would they only send 5 ICBMs instead of launching everything. So, he decided to tell his superiors that the alarm was a mistake and that they should wait for further reports from the Arctic radar stations.

After a nail-biting long while, the reports came back and revealed that there were no ICBMS that came from the USA. It was a system error.

One man's judgment versus a computer saved the world that day.

You type in a post and share it with your thousands of followers on social media or so you think that is indeed the scale of your network. Then you check your analytics and see that it has only reached hundreds. You might ask yourself: what is going on? As it turns out, your post has actually been reviewed for relevance. The algorithm judges it for you before deciding if your network should see it.

If you think that this is in China, nope, it is not. This is happening on major US social media platforms. Add this to the fact that, according to Kepios, there are around 5.07 billion social media users around the world at the start of April 2024 or about 62% percent of the world's population. This is a massive judgment call that the algorithm makes for you. If you look at the known data of the social media industry, which has a value of about US$ 251.45 billion, you would realize the sector has a lot of money and is one of the reasons why the demand for data centers is growing.

In a thought-provoking TED Talk: The Next Global Superpower Isn't Who You Think, Ian Bremmer said:

But today, our identities are determined by nature and nurture and algorithms. If you want to challenge the system, you can't just question authority, as we were all told when we were growing up. Today, you have to question the algorithm, which is a staggering amount of power in the hands of these technology companies. What are they going to do with that power? And that depends on who they want to be when they grow up.

There is a growing blurring of lines between the online censorship of governments like China to technology companies like Facebook and LinkedIn. Every piece of content is intensely reviewed to determine what to say and what not to say.

With the emergence of generative AI and more computing powers, where we spend more money on teaching computers how to think more than education, this is another seismic shift.

Generative AI is poised to become a US$ 1.3 trillion market by 2032, according to a headline in Bloomberg. What is also clear is the growing chasm between those who can afford the infrastructure for data and AI versus those who can't.

Being involved in the data center business, I can see firsthand how much the industry is dependent on talent, energy, and capital to build data centers that can support this monstrosity. At a data center trade fair in 2023, it was mind-boggling for me to see a China Mobile map where many of the submarine data cables in Southeast Asia converge mainly in Singapore. And I couldn't help but wonder, why does one of the world's smallest states hold so much of these cables? The answer is, again, good governance and talent that supports ecosystem but states that do not have these will eventually lose out.

With the convergence of powerful chips and AI, robotics is becoming part and parcel of everyday life. With robots able to recharge on their own and gain autonomy, and probably even agency, it is a certainty that technology will have enormous implications for humanity.

While we intentionally surrender so much of our know-how to a largely untested system, how do we know if it will work? Will we even be allowed to say no to a system failure if one were to happen like in the case of Colonel Petrov?

Nonetheless, we have to be prepared to match up to the vision we create because in a decade, a lot of this will become mature enough to dictate the shape of the future.

The next dictator may be one we cannot see.

SPACE –
Many Moons, One Earth

With the earth shaking and debris flying, the Indian-built *Mangalyaan* (Mars craft in English) was launched towards Mars. The mission became a success and Mangalyaan operated for seven and a half years, studying Martian landscapes and their composition.

From Satish Dhawan to Cape Canaveral, the space age is back again. Total government spending on the space industry is rising to US$ 117 billion in 2023 and the market size is valued at US$ 443.20 billion in 2023. By 2033, it is expected to reach close to a trillion.

Elon Musk's tenacity and business acumen have paved the way for a new generation of startups to follow suit in search of gold in the new space rush. SpaceX is estimated to be worth US$ 180 billion based on secondary share sale, according to CNBC in December 2023

Musk has an even larger rocket he wants to deploy with the aim of conquering Mars. The potential of that happening is getting closer. To get there quicker, Musk has been testing rockets to evaluate areas for improvement. That is one big bet.

Other billionaires are also in the space race with him, although in different versions. Jeff Bezos believes in putting heavy industries on the moon and other planets to take it out of planet Earth. Landing on comets to collect samples for research also seems to be a walk in the park nowadays. Hence, asteroid mining has seriously become a thing now.

According to a study by Ian Lange of the Colorado School of Mines, depending on clean energy transition, mineral prices, lowering of space launch prices, and amount of capital and R&D growth, the production of some metals from space can overtake production on Earth in 30 to 40 years. This is because metallic asteroids contain more than a thousand times as much nickel as the Earth's crust, in terms of grams per metric ton and have significant cobalt, iron, platinum, and other metal concentrations.

Both the U.S. and China have declared plans to set up lunar stations on the moon. The U.S. hopes to do so by 2028 to begin the first phase of setting up a lunar base. China has the same deadline, too. Both are recruiting countries and partners to join their respective projects.

With the amount of time, alliances, and resources, you can be certain that within a decade, mining on comets will no longer be science fiction. This will change our relationship with the stars when it becomes easier to hop onto the next destination. The moon.

But since the technology to reach Alpha Centauri is still elusive, we can still only call the Earth our home. For now. However, we can certainly find many moons along the way to support planet Earth in the near future.

The Four Horsemen

This second set of trends is what I call the **Four Futures of Doom or The Four Horsemen**.

In the Book of Revelations, the four horsemen were depicted to herald the end of the world. I am not here to preach about the end of the world as I am not a theologian, so I am not about to go into an exegesis of that. However, I do see four intentional trends of doom that are avoidable but if unstopped will be cataclysmic to society. They are:

1. **Extremism Leadership**

The rise of leaders who are only good with public relations or social media is devastating. Nowadays, it is more about shock-value to make a statement. When leadership is about all grandstanding, people suffer across the board. These are leaders with a lot of power, so this dramatically increases the risk of nuclear war, economic malaise, and so on.

2.   End of Trusted Institutions

The idea of an institution is so hated and opposed that it has become a dangerous trend. It takes a lot of hard work to make any institution work and dictators rise when there are no systems in place to hold them accountable. This subsequently decreases trust in the system since credibility is lost.

3.   Extremism Economics

Capitalism used to work. But with the growing chasm between rich and poor, it is no longer a feasible system. Furthermore, the changing dynamics of the job market due to technology will also affect us in more ways than one.

4.   End of Education

Schools and universities used to be hubs for change. However, education has become overtly commercialized which has overtaken its cause in generating values-driven women and men to change the world. There is an urgency to change education for impact.

Let me explain further in the next four threads.

Extremism Leadership –
A Grandstanding Tower of Babel

It was written that ancient Babylonians wanted to build a mighty tower for their glory and to impress the world. It was going to be so tall it could reach the heavens. Seeing their pride, God decided to disrupt their work by confusing the language of the workers which halted the project and dispersed people to the ends of the earth. The tower became known as Babel, which means "to confuse."

Today, even though there is incredible technology to help us connect, God does not need to confuse us anymore. Our world leaders are more than capable of sowing confusion themselves. This is further fueled by so many grandstanding statements about how to make respective nations great again that drives people into extremist positions. Hate speech is increasingly peddled by political leaders as researched by different experts.

Hate speech has also figured prominently in the recent rhetoric of political leaders in a variety of countries including Russia, Colombia, Israel, Egypt, Ukraine, the Philippines, Italy, Greece, Sri Lanka and Iraq.

- James Piazza, Liberal Arts Professor of Political Science, Penn State University

The ongoing wars, from Gaza to Ukraine, are all justified by uncompromising positions of one or the other which results limited room to dialogue for lasting peace, the threat of more wars is looming on other shores, such as the Taiwan Straits or the South China Sea, if leaders continue their grandstanding and take things to the extreme.

When I was in Lindau in 2019 for the unveiling of a sculpture for peace, an imam from Bosnia passionately implored:

"Why do we dialogue? We dialogue not just for others but for ourselves, to exorcize our inner demons to be a better human being!"

Indeed, we need leaders of dialogue, not extremists, to exorcize the many demons that threaten world peace.

On 4 February 2019, Pope Francis and Sheikh Ahmed el-Tayeb, Grand Imam of Al-Azhar, met in Abu Dhabi to launch a visionary co-authored document called the *Document for*

Human Fraternity for World Peace and Living Together. It sets out an ambitious outline to nurture dialogue and to opt instead for creative solutions towards human fraternity.

It was a historic moment as these two leaders represent global religions with a history of trying to cancel each other out to the point of armed conflict. This document inspired the United Nations to declare the International Day of the Human Fraternity. Interestingly, the Timor Leste government voted to incorporate the principles of the document into its school curriculum in 2022.

Conversely, the deficit of values-led leadership is troubling.

At Lindau, situated in the calm lake of Constance in Bundsee, the beautiful sculpture which was launched is aptly named Ring for Peace. Designed by Gisbert Baarmann, the 7.5 m-high standing wooden ring takes the form of a Möbius strip. The ring consists of 36 woods of certified cultivation from all continents—a perfect symbol of the constant and integrative nature of dialogue as part of human consciousness.

The crisis of today needs to be led by a new generation of creative leadership capable of dialogue, and systematic engagement to build peace in politics and the economy.

There will be a lot to cover about leadership, so my partner, Jim Funk, and I will contribute to this discourse by presenting an approach which we will explore in greater detail through another book scheduled for 2025.

The End of Trusted Institutions – Death to Congress

Passing through colonnades, entering ornate rooms, and filming themselves on social media with pride on their faces, the storming of the US Congress shocked the world.

I wondered what the founding fathers of the United States would have thought about this. This is not a government of absolute power but of duly elected representatives. And worse, they were called to arms by a president who felt aggrieved by the electoral results.

What the founding fathers of the US feared is happening 245 years after the founding of the republic.

But what is happening in the US is not new. Entrepreneurs of new currency seeking to raise money cast conspiracy doubts on banks to raise billions. Many politicians attack their institutions to justify change. In the extreme case of the cultural revolution in China, where all institutions and institutional knowledge were considered evil, that genie seems to have come out of the bottle and infected everyone.

In a climate where trust is low in institutions all the time, this will be a foundational challenge for humanity. According to Gallup's annual update on trust in government institutions and actors, Americans have the most faith in local government (67%) and the least faith in the legislative branch of the federal government, or Congress (32%). The growing distrust in the idea of large institutions is a concern.

This is problematic mainly because the ability of human beings to organize at scale comes from having institutions. Now, increasingly institutions have become a bad thing. When people are asked what else they can come up with, people dangerously assume that without organization, things will be better.

There is a tendency towards holacracy—a decentralized form of decision-making that empowers employees—and, along the way, boosting innovation by reducing bureaucratic barriers and red tape. So, in practice, does it really work when adults are trusted to do their own thing?

Zappos was one of the first large-size firms to try holacracy but it became distracting and unwieldy after a while. Zappos executive John Bunch explained that the company encountered big challenges in its business metrics as holacracy became too internal instead of being focused on the customer.

History has repeatedly proven that civilizations that can best organize themselves in terms of institutions win. One big factor for the rise of the United States is the design of its institutions. It was not only about freedom of speech but an organized system of thought with carefully designed steps from the judiciary to the separation of powers between the President, Congress, and so on. The fact that the institutions of the United States continue to stand despite a painful civil war and the repeated challenges in recent years, proves its resilience.

In a way, it is similar to the resilience of the Catholic Church because it evolved its institutional model to survive external threats to its existence or even those from internal, such as corruption and division among Christians.

The deeper issue is not to do away with institutions but how to update the model for institutions. Pope Francis is the latest to try and adopt a new institutional model for the church called the synodal process (which means to walk together). This is a way to overcome clericalism and strengthen co-responsibility but it is facing strong resistance.

Lee Kuan Yew, in a speech in 1984 to parliament while advocating a constant update to the way institutions are run, said this:

"The Singapore experience is very recent history. It has worked. Whether it will continue to work depends on getting able, honest and dedicated men to run the system,

able to produce, able to achieve effective goals and make economic progress.

The foundations of this political superstructure - Houses of Parliament, one chamber, two chambers, Houses of Congress, House of Representatives, Senate - they are founded on the infrastructure, the foundations of a society, the state of economic, social and cultural development of a people.

You do not just transfer a Congress and a Constitution and give you a Speaker's Chair and a mace and you have got a Parliament.

It depends on a people's history - their traditions, their national cohesiveness or lack thereof their educational levels, their professional knowledge their industrial skills - whether they feel that they are a nation that they belong to each other, that they are prepared to fight for each other, work with each other, share one destiny.

The rest, the superstructure without this foundation, the infrastructure, are just so much bric-a-brac, like Lego bricks. When the European powers and the Americans transferred these superstructures modeled on their forms, like the Belgian to the Congo, they failed in the Third World."

In a crisis like the end of institutions, we need good men and women willing to put in the effort and strength to rebuild them again, this time differently.

Extremism Economy –
An Intransigent Economic System
in Need of an Upgrade

"I've always been deeply opposed to crypto, bitcoin [...]
The only true use case for it is criminals, drug traffickers
[...] money laundering, tax avoidance [...] If I was the
government, I'd close it down."

- Jamie Dimon, CEO of JP Morgan in the U.S. Senate
Banking, Housing and Urban Affairs Committee oversight,
6 Dec 2023 Capitol Hill in Washington, D.C.

Everything happens for a reason, including the rise of cryptocurrency. The shift towards cryptocurrency has been largely due to mistrust in existing financial institutions and the 2008 crisis proved the conspiracy theorists right: banks are not here for customers, they are here to scam you. Hence, a decentralized network where digital currency is secured by cryptography started to make sense.

This is a contest for legitimacy and trust.

Written off as a non-value, crypto's value has been rather resilient despite setbacks and major scandals. In May 2024, Binance founder Changpeng Zhao was handed a sentence of four months in prison. This starkly contrasts with the 25-year prison sentence FTX's Sam Bankman-Fried received. The nature crimes of both men differed greatly; Zhao was more concerned with regulatory compliance, while Bankman-Fried was downright fraudulent. Zhao and Bankman-Fried have been known adversaries as well as critical stewards of the US$ 2.2 trillion crypto sector.

Yes, you read it correctly. Crypto is that big right now.

After the 2008 financial crisis happened, many economists and business leaders have called for a change in the current economic system, as it is no longer effective in giving access to uplift people from poverty.

This is why I describe the current state of the economy as an "Extremism Economy." It is extremist because the current system is designed to benefit the wealthiest and denies the middle class from growth. As a result of deep distrust, people have increasingly expressed their preference to have their wealth outside of the system through crypto or cash, for example. India tried to snuff out the black market money through the demonetization exercise in 2016 but failed to achieve its goal and hurt the economy instead.

In 2021, Jeffrey Sachs, an economist who advocates for equitable development, argued for why the economy needs to be redesigned:

> "At last month's COP26 climate summit, hundreds of financial institutions declared that they would put trillions of dollars to work to finance solutions to climate change. Yet a major barrier stands in the way: The world's financial system actually impedes the flow of finance to developing countries, creating a financial death trap for many.
>
> Economic development depends on investments in three main kinds of capital:
>
> - Human capital (health and education)
> - Infrastructure (power, digital, transport, and urban)
> - Businesses

Poorer countries have lower levels per person of each kind of capital, and therefore also have the potential to proliferate by investing in a balanced way across them. These days, that growth can and should be green and digital, avoiding the high-pollution growth of the past."

In my view, structural and systemic faults in the current economic system are a consequence of a deeper form of poverty in the world and it is in three aspects:

Poverty of Trust: Without trust, there will be no sharing of vulnerability and no sharing of needs or goods. This is seen in the issue with crypto where people do not trust the existing system that is why they need to lean on alternatives or non-mainstream channels.

Poverty of Institutions: There are insufficient institutions to work towards ending of extreme poverty or help to expand the growth of the middle class.

Poverty of Solutions: This is the absence of systemic solutions to bridge the different divides in the economic system, entrenching the current state towards poverty.

This is why the fundamental call by Chiara Lubich in 1991 to bring about a new form of economy that is based on human fraternity, called the Economy of Communion (EoC), makes sense. Without first recognizing human dignity and the need to grow the economy for the common good, we can never have a system that works for all. Communism failed as it is just another form of extremism. What we need is an updated economic system.

There are many things to discuss about the economy, and this has been Consulus' core mission—to realize an Economy of Communion. However, the conversation on this topic warrants another book to deepen the discourse and promote common action.

End of Education –
Death by Bureaucracy and Status Quo

Over a warm bowl of beef noodles, the best that Kaohsiung can offer, and a Taiwanese beer, I sat beside Mei Fei and I-Chen, both lecturers from Wenzao University. It was an intense day of discussions on how to roll out a new purpose statement, which is about helping students discover their purpose and mission for the betterment of Taiwanese society.

Mei Fei asked me, "Hey Lawrence, we are so fixated on the students about their purpose, do you think we should ask the teachers, too? How sure are we that they are clear about their purpose and mission?"

I was stumped, and I totally agree. Also, because we tend to be so focused on educational outcomes, we forget about the enablers themselves. But this also got me thinking about our broader work with universities from the US, Italy, and Asia—what is actually going on?

The modern Western University came from medieval schools known as Studia Generalia which were centers of learning open to all parts of Europe. But from the 9th century onwards, the spaces of learning rose out of the need to educate clerks and monks beyond cathedral and monastic schools. Yes, you heard it right. Schools in Europe were originally part of cathedrals, as such, a student has to undergo spiritual and moral development in addition to personal competency.

Fast forward to today's universities, the global education sector is a huge market valued at US$ 736.80 billion in 2023. It has its own set of rules, status, and bureaucracy which also meant the cost of maintaining a university is very expensive. This meant that commercial interests had to take precedence. Hence, spiritual and moral development have also become far less important.

The aim of getting an education is to get a degree to secure a good job. But even this expected outcome is no longer a guarantee as millions of graduates need help finding work. In China, for example, a lot of graduates struggle to secure employment.

As of March 2024, it is estimated that about 15.3% of young people cannot find work. Many of them come from universities that are merely interested in producing graduates but not effective persons who can join the workforce.

Education, in general, is facing unprecedented challenges because for years, it has become a system with a set of practices that seemingly cannot be questioned. Several CEOs no longer believe in the relevance of the current education model.

Richard Branson, who was featured in a CNBC article in 2018, said that schools are failing to teach the necessary skills that are needed in the business world because they have such rigid guidelines. According to him:

"Many children are set up to fail by a system that only cares about exam results [...] I want to see education reimagined to support creative minds and alternative thinkers [...] I want to see possibilities explored and children having adventures."

Another CEO who shares the view that education is broken is Elon Musk, who said:

"The way teaching more typically works is we're going to teach you a course on screwdrivers and a course on wrenches."

The other major challenge is that the private sector is now coming up with a more compelling vision and digital methods to educate kids. The top players in the so-called Learning Management Systems (LMS) category are Google Classroom with 11.37%, LinkedIn Learning with 10%, Moodle with 8.79%, and TalentLMS with a 5.54% market share. Hence, educational institutions, especially those funded by the government, may not have the resources or the entrepreneurial skills to challenge the rise of such platforms.

Then, there is the rise of generative AI, which will throw a lot of the fundamental work of education into question.

However, the most significant challenge whenever we work with universities ourselves is that there is a whole set of existing university playbooks that are almost untouchable. It is a fixed set of practices for ranking, curriculum development, and operating model. The bolder the idea, the harder it is to implement. Because the fastest way to introduce any new program is to follow precedents, or else it is hard to proceed. And when I asked why? The answer is always, "This is the way it has always been. Bear with us."

In an age of seismic change, for a sector that is supposed to help students become braver in navigating the new world, too many educational institutions seem unwilling to find the courage to fulfill their promise. And so in an AI age, we need a new model of schools that intergrate all the way into higher learning, with greater emphasis on values, wisdom

and creativity. We need to shape an inspired next generation that knows how to use technology with wisdom. To give
them hope and not fill them with dread for the new age. This
has to be our collective responsibility as Changemakers.

These last nine threads were written with my daughter, Natalia, in mind, who is about to turn nine this year.

As a father, I am frightened at the growing number of issues that society continues to face both in online and offline spaces. The youth will be the ones to face the repercussions of corrupt systems and the abuse perpetrated by those in positions of power.

However, I am still hopeful that despite the state of the world, unlike before, there are a growing number of Changemakers who will rise up to the occasion to face wind and fire, and turn the wheel of the change cycle to pursue the change they wish to see in the world.

The Heart of Lasting Change

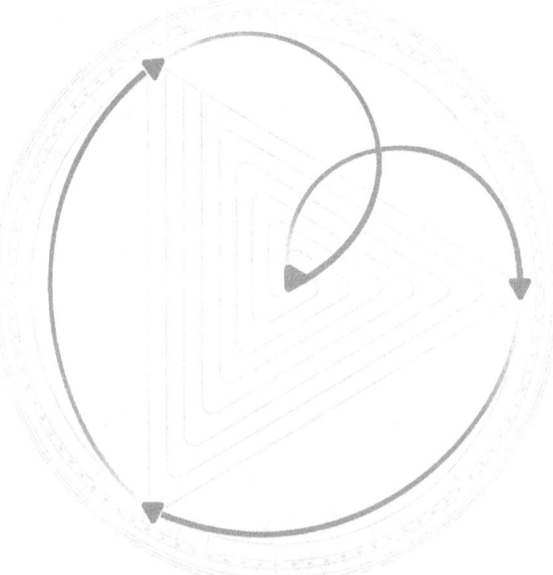

If you have read from start to end or have only read the parts that are most relevant to you, I thank you for the privilege of your time. I hope I have aided your cause in a small way, helped you anchor that creative vision that was always in your mind, encouraged you to appreciate the people around you, and nudged you to make that timely pivot competently.

Ultimately, I hope that you see why it is important for all of us to see beyond and succeed, too. These words and time spent are worth nothing if we do not bring the change we are meant to see and bring.

From the examples and personal experiences, I hope I have done justice to bring a broad spectrum of actors who have shaped our world for good (or some not that good) and highlight the lessons we can take away from their stories. Whether the Changemaker is in a tech firm or in the field planting a tree, I want us to look at the issues deeper and wider because change is just so hard. But it is not impossible if we put our heart into it.

I have met and continue to meet inspiring Changemaker friends from around the world, and I have come to realize that if a calling is the change we are meant to bring, we will become that person to deliver. The certainty of that calling will be manifested in the rise of a movement that will follow us and provide us with the resources to do what is needed.

Come what may, whatever crisis there might be, Changemakers will always rise to the challenge so long as they find the heart of lasting change.

ACKNOWLEDGMENTS

Thank you

I thank God for the gift of an extraordinary life and calling.

To Chiara Lubich, I am deeply grateful for your cause towards building a united world

To Michelle, the love of my life, you help me start again whenever I fall, thank you.

To my little Natalia, this is written for you, may you find your Everest.

To my fellow Changemaker Consulites, thank you for co-creating with me this vision. To Vincent Chee for spearheading the design; to Paul Matangcas for editing the ebb and flow of the words; to Rusdi Budiman for being a good critic and checker; to Rebecca Teo for her leadership in challenging my assumptions and critical efforts in indexing the book; to Kannon Kwan for being patient in driving this til the end; and to Rawi Ahmed for getting the print and production sorted.

To all Consulites who patiently inspired me to do this, like Helena Pham, yes, it is here. Jim Funk, Shiraz Latiff, and Stanislav Lencz, thank you for the deep conversations. Special thanks to Jeffrey Chiu and Rawi Ahmed, my partners at the firm. This would not have happened without you saying yes to change the world.

To the book circle for your insights, thoughts, and comments. You guided me like a sherpa and encouraged me during the arduous climb, especially during moments when I nearly fell off the project. So thank you Albert Kong, Alexander Lau, Ang Miah Khiang, Ashima Thomas, Azril Mohd Amin, Abhi Kumar, Antonia Carla Testa, Caroline Haddad, Clara Kwan, Colin Thoms, Dylan Yee, Francis Yap, Gino Bulan, Hrvoje Lovrić, Kuan Chee Yung, Jeelian Leong, Jim Funk, Jonathan Eng, Lawrence Peh, Tong Mingxi, Rebecca Teo, Simon Ong, Shivaun Goh, Shiraz Latiff, Nurul a Jaafar, Paolo Frizzi, Radin Sufri, Rofina Tham Su Eing, Stanislav Lencz, Theresa Sze Ying Goh, Ulrich Schraudolph, Vincent Chee.

The book circle provided feedback before the writing of this book but did not review its development, so I alone bear responsibility for the content I wrote in this book.

Special thanks to Mohammad Imtiaz Hossain who helped vet my experience in Dhaka. To Ujwal Raj Gautam who helped with the phrase in Nepali. To my Brother, Dr. Andrew Kwasari for the experience in Africa and the quote in Hausa language.

To those who left their comments on my TEDx video, your questions and comments were like bright stars that guided me when I was lost.

Thank you to all the Changemakers who have inspired me throughout my life.

THREAD GUIDES

The idea of using threads to structure the narrative of this book was inspired by Chiara Lubich, who once said that we are all threads, part of a beautiful tapestry.

I remember standing in awe in the 800-foot-long corridor of the Vatican Gallery of Tapestries, or Galleria degli Arazzi, and seeing massive tapestries of historic events made from wool, silk, silver, and gold threads.

I wrote these 80 threads hoping they can contribute to the tapestry of change that you are weaving in your life.

This section is written to make it easier for you to find any thread that inspired you.

PART ONE: SEEING

PART FIVE: COMPETENT PIVOT

PART SIX: SEEING BEYOND

BIBLIOGRAPHY

EPIGRAPH

Apple Inc. (1997). Think different [Advertisement].

Richter, Irma. A (1952). *Leonardo da Vinci Notebooks*. Oxford University Press

INTRODUCTION

Stein, Vickly. (2023). Goldilocks zone: Everything you need to know about the habitable sweet spot. Space. https://www.space.com/goldilocks-zone-habitable-area-life

Bremmer, Ian. (2013). Ian Bremmer: The Problem with Global Leadership Today. Diplomatic Courier. https://www.diplomaticourier.com/posts/ian-bremmer-the-problem-with-global-leadership-today

Davies, Rob. (2018). Apple becomes world's first trillion-dollar company. Guardian. https://www.theguardian.com/technology/2018/aug/02/apple-becomes-worlds-first-trillion-dollar-company

Vasagar, Jeevan. (2017). Singapore-on-Thames? This is no vision for post-Brexit Britain. Guardian. https://www.theguardian.com/commentisfree/2017/nov/24/singapore-on-thames-post-brexit-britain-wealthy-city-state

Chong, Lawrence. (2022). How your Strategy can be Great by Design. TED. https://www.ted.com/talks/lawrence_chong_how_your_strategy_can_be_great_by_design

MY CHANGEMAKER JOURNEY

Johnson, Becky A. (2010). Faith in Action: Working toward the Millennium Development Goals. Religions for Peace. https://rfp.org/sites/default/files/pubications/MDG%20Religious%20Toolkit%20-%202nd%20edition.pdf

Thompson, Catherine. (2018). The Case for Funding Peacebuilding. The New Humanitarian. https://deeply.thenewhumanitarian.org/peacebuilding/community/2018/05/21/the-case-for-funding-peacebuilding

AML Intelligence. (2024). LATEST: More than $3trillion in illicit funds flowed through global financial system in 2023; banks call for more regulatory guidance to tackle endemic. https://www.amlintelligence.com/2024/01/latest-more-than-3trillion-in-illicit-funds-flowed-thru-global-financial-system-in-2023-banks-call-for-more-regulatory-guidance-to-tackle-endemic/

UNESCO. (n.d.). UNESCO Prize for Peace Education 1996. https://unesdoc.unesco.org/ark:/48223/pf0000108989

Economy of Communion. (n.d.). What is the EOC?. https://eocnoam.org/what-is-the-eoc/

Riley, Charles. (2017). McKinsey drawn into South Africa's sprawling corruption scandal. CNN. https://money.cnn.com/2017/09/19/news/south-africa-mckinsey-kpmg-gupta/index.html

Choudhury, Ambereen et al. (2023). McKinsey and Its Peers Are Facing the Wildest Headwinds in Years. Bloomberg. https://www.bloomberg.com/news/features/2023-11-22/mckinsey-and-its-consulting-industry-peers-face-the-wildest-headwinds-in-years

Fortune. (2012). Bain: A consulting firm too hot to handle? (Fortune, 1987). https://fortune.com/2012/01/15/bain-a-consulting-firm-too-hot-to-handle-fortune-1987/

Belot, Henry. (2023). Boston Consulting Group accused in Senate inquiry of securing contract extension through 'cosy relations' with officials. Guardian. https://www.theguardian.com/australia-news/2023/sep/26/boston-consulting-group-accused-in-senate-inquiry-of-securing-contract-extension-through-cosy-relations-with-officials

Smallteacher, Richard. (2020). BCG, McKinsey & PwC Consultants Implicated in Angola Corruption Scandal. Corpwatch. https://www.corpwatch.org/article/bcg-mckinsey-pwc-consultants-implicated-angola-corruption-scandal

Consultancy. (2023). Police raid Portugal offices of BCG and PwC in corruption probe. https://www.consultancy.eu/news/amp/8446/police-raid-portugal-offices-of-bcg-and-pwc-in-corruption-probe

Belleuz, Julia. (2021). The World Health Organization broke its own rules to spend millions on BCG consultants. Vox. https://www.vox.com/2021/6/16/22527665/world-health-organization-who-12-million-bcg-consultants

Holey, Stephen. (2024). US consulting firms accused of withholding information on Saudi ties. Financial Times. https://www.ft.com/content/f2938a10-39bb-4040-a786-00bc98e03061

The Irish Times. (2024). McKinsey and BCG warn staff face jail if they reveal Saudi work. https://www.irishtimes.com/business/2024/02/07/mckinsey-and-bcg-warn-staff-face-jail-if-they-reveal-saudi-work/

Khadem, Nassim. (2023). Review of PwC tax leaks scandal will not stop conflicts of interest engulfing consulting firms. ABC News. https://amp.abc.net.au/article/102904272

PART ONE: SEEING – A LION'S GAZE

Thread 1

Chong, Lawrence. (2022). How your Strategy can be Great by Design. TED. https://www.ted.com/talks/lawrence_chong_how_your_strategy_can_be_great_by_design

Thread 2

Bremmer, Ian. (2023). The Next Global Superpower Isn't Who You Think. TED. https://www.ted.com/talks/ian_bremmer_the_next_global_superpower_isn_t_who_you_think?language=en

Thread 3

Fair, James. (2023). Deadliest apex predators in the wild: which mammals are the best killing machines?. Discover Wild Life. https://www.discoverwildlife.com/animal-facts/mammals/hunting-success-rates-how-predators-compare

Thread 4

Walton, Calder. (2022). What's Old Is New Again: Cold War Lessons for Countering Disinformation. Texas National Security Review. https://tnsr.org/2022/09/whats-old-is-new-again-cold-war-lessons-for-countering-disinformation/

Cox, William T.L. (2022). Untested assumptions perpetuate stereotyping: Learning in the absence of evidence. Science Direct. https://www.sciencedirect.com/science/article/pii/S0022103122000993?via%3Dihub

Funk, Allie et al. (n.d.). The Repressive Power of Artificial Intelligence. Freedom House. https://freedomhouse.org/report/freedom-net/2023/repressive-power-artificial-intelligence

Campbell, Dakin. (2023). How WeWork went from a $47 billion valuation to a basket case in just 6 weeks. Business Insider. https://www.businessinsider.com/weworks-nightmare-ipo

Thread 5

Issacson, Walter. (2017). Leonardo da Vinci. Simon & Schuster

Thread 6

Hope, Bradley. Emshwiller, John R. Fritz, Ben (2016) The Secret Money Behind 'The Wolf of Wall Street' https://www.wsj.com/articles/malaysias-1mdb-the-secret-money-behind-the-wolf-of-wall-street-1459531987

Boyle, Darren. (2016).(2016). 'This is a case where life imitated art:' US Justice Department claims Wolf of Wall Street film was financed with $100m of laundered cash from Malaysia.

Tau, Byron. (2023). Leonardo DiCaprio Testifies at Pras Michel's 1MDB Trial. The Wall Street Journal. https://www.wsj.com/articles/leonardo-dicaprio-testifies-at-pras-michels-1mdb-trial-ef097fd

Azhar, Daniel. (2024). Malaysia has recovered $4.8 mln in 1MDB assets since Jan 2023. Reuters. https://www.reuters.com/business/malaysia-recovers-over-4-mln-1mdb-assets-between-2023-feb-2024-2024-02-08/

Metz, Cade. (2023). The Fear and Tension That Led to Sam Altman's Ouster at OpenAI. NY Times. https://www.nytimes.com/2023/11/18/technology/open-ai-sam-altman-what-happened.html

Thread 7

National Public Radio. (2011). Occupy Wall Street Inspires Worldwide Protests. https://www.npr.org/2011/10/15/141382468/occupy-wall-street-inspires-worldwide-protests

Barron, James & Moynihan, Colin. (2011). City Reopens Park After Protesters Are Evicted. The New York Times. https://www.nytimes.com/2011/11/16/nyregion/police-begin-clearing-zuccotti-park-of-protesters.html

Consulus. (n.d). Unify Methodology. https://consulus.com/about-4/unify-methodology/

Euro News. (2023). From solo protest to global movement: Five years of Fridays for Future in pictures. https://www.euronews.com/green/2023/08/21/from-solo-protest-to-global-movement-five-years-of-fridays-for-future-in-pictures

Thread 8

Lee, Kuan Yew. (1998). The Singapore Story: Memoirs of Lee Kuan Yew. Prentice Hall

Menon, Ravi. (2015). An Economic History of Singapore: 1965-2065. Monetary Authority of Singapore. https://www.mas.gov.sg/news/speeches/2015/an-economic-history-of-singapore

CIMSEC. (2018). The decisive fleet engagement at the battle of the Yalu river. https://cimsec.org/the-decisive-fleet-engagement-at-the-battle-of-the-yalu-river/

Edwards, Jim. (2017). 500 years ago, China destroyed its world-dominating navy because its political elite was afraid of free trade. Independent. ERindependent.co.uk/news/world/americas/500-years-ago-china-destroyed-its-worlddominating-navy-because-its-political-elite-was-afraid-of-free-trade-a7612276.html

Banker, Steve. (2024). Boeing Is Haunted By Two Decades Of Outsourcing. Forbes. https://www.forbes.com/sites/stevebanker/2024/02/12/boeing-is-haunted-by-two-decades-of-outsourcing/?sh=2a9b2d7064a1

Useem, Jerry. (2024). Boeing and the Dark Age of American Manufacturing. The Atlantid. https://www.theatlantic.com/ideas/archive/2024/04/boeing-corporate-america-manufacturing/678137/

Thread 9

Heiney, Anna C. (2023). The 1980s: All Eyes Focus on Space Shuttle. NASA. https://www.nasa.gov/history/the-1980s-all-eyes-focus-on-space-shuttle/

Zhou, Li. (2023). An oil executive is leading the UN climate summit. It's going as well as you'd expect. Vox. https://www.vox.com/climate/2023/12/4/23988430/cop28-climate-fossil-fuels-jaber

WHO. (2019). 1 in 3 people globally do not have access to safe drinking water- UNICEF. WHO. https://www.who.int/news/item/18-06-2019-1-in-3-people-globally-do-not-have-access-to-safe-drinking-water-unicef-who

Khalil, Ashraf. (2022). Jon Stewart: Authoritarian governments a threat, not comedy. AP News. https://apnews.com/article/bill-cosby-entertainment-arts-and-talk-shows-dave-chappelle-eb2362ca7076700492493462e78ab7ca

Statista. (2023). Number of nuclear warheads worldwide as of January 2023. https://www.statista.com/statistics/264435/number-of-nuclear-warheads-worldwide/

Investopedia. (2024). Black Swan in the Stock Market: What Is It, With Examples and History. https://www.investopedia.com/terms/b/blackswan.asp

Thread 10

Hibakusha's stories. (n.d.). Who are The Hikabusha?. https://hibakushastories.org/who-are-the-hibakusha/

Araya, Danial. (2024). The Nuclear Age Has Only Just Begun. Centre for International Governance Innovation. https://www.cigionline.org/articles/the-nuclear-age-has-only-just-begun/

[Fortune Magazine]. (2017, Mar 22). How These Companies Did a Total Restart for the Sake of Innovation [Video]. Youtube. https://www.youtube.com/watch?v=gJtK12HZpgg

Thread 11

Schwab, Klaus. (2019). Our global system has spun out of control. Here's how to rebalance it. World Economic Forum. https://www.weforum.org/agenda/2019/02/how-to-rebalance-our-global-system/

Thorpe, Emma. (2022). Blue Origin Vs SpaceX: The Hard Race To Space Leadership. Orbital Today. https://orbitaltoday.com/2022/04/19/blue-origin-vs-spacex-the-hard-race-to-space-leadership/

Thread 12

Weinberger, Matt and Hartmans, Avery (2024). Steve Jobs' life and Apple career, from cofounder, to exile, to CEO. Business Insider. https://www.businessinsider.com/steve-jobs

Lee, Kuan Yew. (2000). From Third World to First: The Singapore Story: 1965-2000. Harper

PART TWO: CAUSE – FINDING YOUR EVEREST

Thread 15

Calaprice, Alice. (2011). The Ultimate Quotable EINSTEIN. Princeton University Press

Thread 16

Sagarmatha Overview. (n.d.). Nepal Himal Peak Profile. Retrieved from https://nepalhimalpeakprofile.org/sagarmatha

The Economist Group (n.d.). Our founding mission. https://www.economistgroup.com/businesses/the-economist

Anti-Slavery International. (2007). Slavery past and present. https://www.antislavery.org/wp-content/uploads/2017/02/slavery_past_and_present.pdf

Burke, Myles. (2023). The fall of the Berlin Wall: The moment that reshaped Europe. BBC. https://www.bbc.com/culture/article/20231108-the-fall-of-the-berlin-wall-the-moment-that-reshaped-europe

Thread 17

Gibbons, Sarah. (2016). Design Critiques: Encourage a Positive Culture to Improve Products. Nielsen Norman Group. https://www.nngroup.com/articles/design-critiques/

Yarow, Jay. (2011). Steve Jobs' Hilarious Response To Larry Ellison's Plan To Buy Apple So They Could Both Get Richer. Business Insider. https://www.businessinsider.com/steve-jobs-larry-ellison-2011-10

Thread 18

Consulus. (2013). Lawrence Chong ends four years of Presidency at Design Business Chamber Singapore. https://consulus.com/lawrence-chong-ends-four-years-of-presidency-at-design-business-chamber-singapore/

Singapore Good Design. (n.d.). About Singapore Good Design. https://sgmark.org/

Thread 19

Cambridge Dictonary. (n.d.). Vocation. https://dictionary.cambridge.org/dictionary/english/vocation

Royle, Orianna Rosa. (2024). Nvidia founder tells Stanford students their high expectations may make it hard for them to succeed: 'I wish upon you ample doses of pain and suffering'. Fortune. https://fortune.com/2024/03/13/nvidia-founder-ceo-jensen_huang-stanford-students-genz-grads-low-expectations-successful/

Thread 20

Jobs, Steve. (2005). 'You've got to find what you love,' Jobs says. Stanford. https://news.stanford.edu/2005/06/12/youve-got-find-love-jobs-says/

Kovach, Steve. (2011). His Other Gig: How Steve Jobs Turned Pixar Into A Billion Dollar Empire. Business Insider. https://www.businessinsider.com/steve-jobs-pixar-2011-10

Kawamoto, Dawn. (1996). Apple acquires Next, Jobs. CNETS. https://www.cnet.com/tech/tech-industry/apple-acquires-next-jobs/

Lee Kuan Yew in 1923-2015. (n.d.). Remembering Lee Kuan Yew. https://www.remembering.gov.sg/life-and-contributions/mr-lee-and-singapore/lee-kuan-yew-1923-2015/

Thread 21

Pullella, Philip. (2023). Pope Benedict was first pontiff to resign in 600 years. Reuters. https://www.reuters.com/world/obituary-former-pope-benedict-was-first-pontiff-resign-600-years-2022-12-31/

Bible Gateway. (n.d.). Matthew 16:24. https://www.biblegateway.com/verse/en/Matthew%2016%3A24

Thread 23

Consulus. (2021). What would a 'Corporate Vaccine for Resilience' look like?. https://consulus.com/what-would-a-corporate-vaccine-for-resilience-look-like-whitepaper/

Thread 24

Focolore's story. (n.d.). Focolare. https://www.focolare.org/en/

Fisher, Ian. (2008). Chiara Lubich, Who Founded Catholic Lay Group, Dies at 88. The New York Times. https://www.nytimes.com/2008/03/15/world/europe/15lubich.html

PART THREE: CREATIVE VISION –
BUILDING YOUR CATHEDRAL

Thread 27

Editors, Charles River. (2016). Frank Lloyd Wright: The Life and Buildings of America's Most Famous Architect. CreateSpace Independent Publishing Platform.

World History Encyclopedia. (2020). Gothic cathedrals: Architecture & divine light. https://www.worldhistory.org/article/1649/gothic-cathedrals-architecture--divine-light/

Isaacson, Walter. (2011). Steve Jobs. Simon & Schuster.

Gallo, Carmine. (2011). Steve Jobs and the power of vision. Forbes. https://www.forbes.com/sites/carminegallo/2011/01/18/steve-jobs-and-the-power-of-vision/?sh=406143c9172b

Thread 28

Dictionary. (n.d.). Prophet. https://www.dictionary.com/browse/prophets%27

Overstreet, Kaley. (2022). The Origins and Evolution of Gothic Architecture. Arch Daily. https://www.archdaily.com/983605/the-origins-and-evolution-of-gothic-architecture

Design Boom. (n.d.). a timeline of new york's tallest buildings, from a wooden observatory to one WTC. https://www.designboom.com/architecture/timeline-new-york-tallest-buildings-wooden-observatory-one-wtc-06-08-2021/

Montag, Ali. (2018). Elon Musk explains his motivation to succeed: "There need to be things that inspire you". CNBC. https://www.cnbc.com/2018/03/16/elon-musk-on-inspiration-and-success.html#:~:text=%22Life%20can%20not%20just%20be,and%20be%20part%20of%20humanity.%22

Thread 29

Chong, Lawrence. (2022). How your Strategy can be Great by Design. TED. https://www.ted.com/talks/lawrence_chong_how_your_strategy_can_be_great_by_design

Curator. (2023). Steve Jobs and The Return to Apple. Leadership Story Bank. https://www.leadershipstorybank.com/steve-jobs-and-the-return-to-apple/

Stein, Stanford. (2021). It's Been Two Decades Since Apple Opened Its First Store. Forbes. https://www.google.com/url?q=https://www.forbes.com/sites/

sanfordstein/2021/05/19/apple-store-turns-twenty/?sh%3D40e9b6731acf&s
a=D&source=docs&ust=1716537176635203&usg=AOvVaw2zIvKnxvrvbW5
w9WMj5dtl

Laskow, Sarah. (2015). We Asked a Cultural Historian: Are Apple Stores
the New Temples?. Atlas Obscura. https://www.atlasobscura.com/articles/
we-asked-a-cultural-historian-are-apple-stores-the-new-temples

Fingas, Roger. (2017). Apple leads brick-and-mortar retail with $5,546
in sales per square foot. Apple Insider. https://appleinsider.com/
articles/17/07/28/apple-leads-brick-and-mortar-retail-with-5546-in-sales-
per-square-foot

Gunther, Cory. (2013). Apple retail stores serve 1 million customers daily,
407 locations worldwide. Slash Gear. https://www.slashgear.com/apple-retail-
stores-serve-1-million-customers-daily-407-locations-worldwide-10285704

Thread 30

Singapore Airline. (n.d.). Our Cabin Crew. https://www.singaporeair.com/
en_UK/sg/flying-withus/our-story/our-cabin-crew/

Ang, Seow Leng. (2022). A Great Way to Fly: The Singapore Airlines Story.
National Library Singapore. https://biblioasia.nlb.gov.sg/vol-18/issue-2/jul-
sep-2022/history-singapore-airlines/

Thread 31

Schwantes, Marcel. (2023). The Reason Apple CEO Tim Cook Chose to
Work for Steve Jobs Comes Down to 7 Words. Inc. https://www.inc.com/
marcel-schwantes/the-reason-apple-ceo-tim-cook-chose-to-work-for-steve-
jobs-comes-down-to-7-words.html

Gurman, Mark. (2018). Apple Becomes First U.S. Company to Hit $1 Trillion
Value. Bloomberg. https://www.bloomberg.com/news/articles/2018-08-02/
apple-becomes-first-u-s-company-to-hit-1-trillion-market-value

Thread 32

Cologne Tourism. (n.d.). Cologne Cathedra's Construction History.
https://www.cologne-tourism.com/arts-culture/sights/cologne-cathedral/
construction-history

Shontell, Alyson. (2014). In 1999, Alibaba's CEO Told Employees 2 Things
They Needed To Do To Be Successful: Beat Americans And Work Longer
Hours. Business Insider. https://www.businessinsider.com/jack-mas-early-
1999-speech-to-alibaba-employees-2014-9

[Bloomberg Origin]. (2014, Sep 8). Alibaba IPO: Jack Ma's Original Sales Pitch
in 1999 [Video]. Youtube. https://www.youtube.com/watch?v=Up9-C4_8dVo

Nieva, Richard & Tam, Donna. (2014). Alibaba's blockbuster IPO: Why you should care about the Chinese giant. CNET. https://www.cnet.com/tech/services-and-software/alibabas-blockbuster-ipo-why-you-should-care/

Business Times. (2017). Alibaba's rise creates 10 billionaires, Jack Ma not included. https://www.businesstimes.com.sg/companies-markets/consumer-healthcare/alibabas-rise-creates-10-billionaires-jack-ma-not-included

Thread 33

MK Ghandi. (n.d.).Mahatma Gandhi and the Bhagavad Gita. https://www.mkgandhi.org/articles/Mahatma-Gandhi-and-the-Bhagavad-Gita.html

Ghandi, Mohandas Karamchand. (1993). Gandhi: An Autobiography- The Story of My Experiments with Truth. Beacon Press

Backhouse, Harry. (2023). India, a Story of Progress. Human Progress. https://humanprogress.org/india-a-story-of-progress/

Thread 34

Bariso, Justin. (2023). Emotionally Intelligent People Use a Brilliant 3-Words. Inc. https://www.inc.com/justin-bariso/emotional-intelligence-how-to-move-on-make-most-use-difficulty.html

Moyer, Melinda Wener. (2023). Lean Into Negative Emotions. It's the Healthy Thing to Do. New York Times. https://www.nytimes.com/2023/04/21/well/mind/negative-emotions-mental-health.html

Buni, Catherine. (2003). The great survivor: Ernest Shackleton. Time. https://content.time.com/time/specials/packages/article/0,28804,1981290_1981354_1981610,00.html

Issacson, Walter. (2023). Elon Musk. Simon & Schuster

Thread 35

[Netflix is a Joke]. (2019, Dec 21). Ronny Chieng Is Baffled By Certain States' Mottos [Video]. Youtube. https://www.youtube.com/watch?v=o62WBI0pBDY

[Consulus]. (2021, June 18). Consulus Global Circle | Companies of Purpose [Video]. Youtube. https://youtu.be/RwJpazR7R2o?si=n_0Vbm_udX7DU7cJ

Lee, Kuan Yew. (1965). Speech of Lee Kuan Yew during debate of parliaments in 27th May 1965. National Archives of Singapore. https://www.nas.gov.sg/archivesonline/data/pdfdoc/lky19650527.pdf

Temasek. (n.d.). Our Portfolio. https://www.temasek.com.sg/en/our-investments/our-portfolio accessed 24 May 2023

Thread 36

Boyo, Sydney. (2024). How the Apple iPhone became one of the best-selling products of all time. CNBC. https://www.cnbc.com/2024/01/27/how-the-apple-iphone-changed-the-world.html

Carr, Austin. (2023). Nokia, Snake and the Sad Reign of a Mobile Phone King. Bloomberg. https://www.bloomberg.com/news/newsletters/2023-10-23/google-s-rise-and-nokia-s-smartphone-fall-from-grace

PART FOUR: CIRCLE OF TRUST – GATHERING YOUR CORE

Thread 39

Hoffman, Bryce. (2015). Leadership Quotes From Washington And Lincoln. Forbes. https://www.forbes.com/sites/brycehoffman/2015/02/16/leadership-quotes-from-washington-and-lincoln/?sh=348fd26f44aa

Thread 40

Roberts, Stuart. (n.d.). How Churchill Waged War. University of Cambridge. https://www.cam.ac.uk/stories/churchill-at-war

Bible. (n.d.). Mark 14:32-52. https://www.bible.com/bible/296/MRK.14.32-52.GNBUK

Wallenstein, Andrew. (2022). Tim Cook, Jony Ive and Laurene Powell Jobs Remember Apple Founder: 'Best Teacher I Ever Had'. Variety. https://variety.com/2022/biz/news/steve-jobs-apple-tim-cook-jony-ive-laurene-powell-code-1235364123/

Ang, Cheng Guan. (2015). Singapore and the Worldview of Lee Kuan Yew. The Diplomat. https://thediplomat.com/2015/03/singapore-and-the-worldview-of-lee-kuan-yew/

Thread 41

Lee, Kuang Yew. (2010). Eulogy by MM Lee Kuan Yew at the State Funeral Service for the Late Dr Goh Keng Swee. Prime Minister's Office of Singapore. https://www.pmo.gov.sg/Newsroom/eulogy-minister-mentor-lee-kuan-yew-state-funeral-service-late-dr-goh-keng-swee

SG101. (n.d.). 1959-1965: Early Economic Strategies. https://www.sg101.gov.sg/economy/surviving-our-independence/1959-1965/

SG101. (n.d.). Jurong: From Swamp to Suburb. https://www.sg101.gov.sg/economy/digging-deeper-case-studies/jurong1/

Yongnian, Zheng & Wong, John. (2012). Goh Keng Swee on China. World Scientific Publishing

Kumar, Sree & Siddique, Sharon. (2010). The Singapore success story: public-private alliance for investment attraction, innovation and export development. Economic Commission for Latin America and Caribbean.

Singapore Department of Statistics. (2023). Singapore's Inward Direct Investment Flows 2023. https://www.singstat.gov.sg/-/media/files/news/fdiinflows2023.ashx

Thread 42

Cartwright, Mark. (2017). Mandate of Heaven. World History. https://www.worldhistory.org/Mandate_of_Heaven/

Roy, Ahana. (2022). The Mandate of Heaven: Then and Now. Organization for Research on China and Asia. https://orcasia.org/public/the-mandate-of-heaven-then-and-now

National Geographic. (n.d.). Imperial China's Dynasties. https://education.nationalgeographic.org/resource/imperial-chinas-dynasties/

Dmitriev, S.V & Kuzmin S.L. (n.d.). Conquest Dynasties of China or Foreign Empires? The Problem of Relation between China, Yuan and Qing. Russian Academy of Sciences, Institute of Oriental Sciences.

Stelzenmüller, Constanze. (2016). Does Brexit portend the end of European unity?. Brookings. https://www.brookings.edu/articles/does-brexit-portend-the-end-of-european-unity/

Mitterrand, Francois. (1989). Speech made to assembly, 5 May 1989. Assembly. http://www.assembly.coe.int/nw/xml/Speeches/Speech-XML2HTML-EN.asp?SpeechID=157&a1=4&p2=2&lang=EN

Delors, Jacques. (1995). Intervention de Jacques Delors devant Le Parlement European- Strasbourg, Le 19 Janvier 1995. European Commision. https://ec.europa.eu/commission/presscorner/detail/en/speech_95_3

European Union. (n.d.). Facts and figures on the life in the European Union. https://european-union.europa.eu/principles-countries-history/key-facts-and-figures/life-eu_en

Pampuro, Amanda. (2024). EU maintains stable GDP while cutting greenhouse gas emissions. Courthouse News Service. https://www.courthousenews.com/eu-maintains-stable-gdp-while-cutting-greenhouse-gas-emissions/

Thread 43

Freeman, Douglas Southall. (1952). Washington's Hardest Decision. The Atlantic. https://www.theatlantic.com/past/politics/presiden/freeman.htm

Maryland State House. (n.d.). George Washington's Resignation. https://msa.maryland.gov/msa/mdstatehouse/html/gwresignation. html#:~:text=When%20told%20by%20the%20American,greatest%20 man%20in%20the%20world.%22

Washington, George. (1976). Farewell Address 1976. National Constitution Center. https://constitutioncenter.org/the-constitution/historic-document-library/detail/george-washington-farewell-address-1796

Thread 44

Fiegerman, Seth. (2012). Apple's Designers Actually Work Together At A Kitchen Table Coming Up With Apple's Next Great Products. Business Insider. https://www.businessinsider.com/apples-designers-literally-work-together-at-a-kitchen-table-coming-up-with-apples-next-great-product-2012-8

Dhani. (2019). Apple vs. Samsung: The Design Patent War Between Two Technology Giants. Sagacious Research. https://sagaciousresearch.com/blog/apple-vs-samsung-design-patent-war-between-technology-giants/

Duhigg, Charles. (2016). What Google Learned From Its Quest to Build the Perfect Team. New York Times. https://www.nytimes.com/2016/02/28/magazine/what-google-learned-from-its-quest-to-build-the-perfect-team.html

Chong, Lawrence. (2023). The Unifying Generation. TEDx. https://www.ted.com/talks/lawrence_chong_the_unifying_generation

Thread 45

Consulus. (2020). Transformation of a Catholic University with Purpose and Unity. https://consulus.com/project/wenzao-university-transformation-of-a-catholic-university-with-purpose-and-unity/

Thread 46

Nobel Prize. (n.d.). Mother Teresa. https://www.nobelprize.org/prizes/peace/1979/teresa/facts/

Missionaries of Charity. (n.d.). Welcome to Missionaries of Charity. https://missionariesofcharity.org/index.html

CNN. (1997). Mother Teresa's work carries on. http://edition.cnn.com/WORLD/9709/08/teresa.charities/

Collins, Terry. (2022). The Life of St. John Baptist de La Salle. Lasalle. https://www.lasalleigbm.org/our-founder-articles/the-life-of-saint-john-baptiste-de-la-salle

Laselle. (n.d.). The International Lasallian Mission. https://www.lasalle.org/en/the-international-lasallian-mission/#:~:text=Today%2C%20the%20great%20De%20La,children%2C%20young%20people%20and%20adults.

Kolodiejchuk, Brian. (2007). Mother Teresa: Come Be My Light: The Private Writings of the Saint of Calcutta. Doubleday Religion.

Thread 47

Morley, Oliver. (2012). UK Government – did we rule the Empire with 4,000 civil servants?. National Archives UK Government. https://blog.nationalarchives.gov.uk/uk-government-did-we-rule-the-empire-with-4000-civil-servants/

Zandt, Florian. (2023). The biggest empire in human histories. Statista. https://www.statista.com/chart/20342/peak-land-area-of-the-largest-empires/

Agenzia Info Salesiana. (n.d.). Statistics of the Catholic Church 2023. https://www.infoans.org/en/sections/good-to-know/item/19312-statistics-of-the-catholic-church-2023

Agenzia Fides. (2023). Vatican- Catholic Church Statistics 2023. https://www.fides.org/en/news/74319-VATICAN_CATHOLIC_CHURCH_STATISTICS_2023

Desilver, Drew. (2018). U.S. population keeps growing, but House of Representatives is same size as in Taft era. PEW Research. https://www.pewresearch.org/short-reads/2018/05/31/u-s-population-keeps-growing-but-house-of-representatives-is-same-size-as-in-taft-era/

Lylwelyn, Rev. Dorian. (2022). Global Christianity: the Future of the Catholic Church. USD Dornsife. https://dornsife.usc.edu/iacs/2022/04/30/global-christianity/

Thread 48

Guglielmo, Connie. (2012). A Steve Jobs Moment That Mattered: Macworld, August 1997. Forbes. https://www.forbes.com/sites/connieguglielmo/2012/10/07/a-steve-jobs-moment-that-mattered-macworld-august-1997/?sh=40f94c383edd

Thread 49

Cavendish, Richard. (2012). The Battle of the Milvian Bridge. History Today. https://www.historytoday.com/archive/battle-milvian-bridge

MacCulloch, Diarmaid. (2009). Christianity: The First Three Thousand Years. Allen Lane

Consulus. (n.d.). Consulus' unify methodology. https://consulus.com/about-4/unify-methodology/

PART FIVE: COMPETENT PIVOT – PIVOTING LIKE A BUTTERFLY

Thread 52

Herbert, Frank. (1965). Dune. Chilton Books

Schaffner, Franklin J. (Director). (1968). Planet of Apes [film]. APJAC Productions

Human Origins. (n.d.). How are humans and monkeys related?

- Frequently Asked Questions. https://humanorigins.si.edu/education/frequently-asked-questions#:

Thread 53

Sarel, Michael. (1997). Growth in East Asia What We Can and What We Cannot Infer. IMF. https://www.imf.org/external/pubs/ft/issues1/

Dixit, Avi. (2022). How the Singapore Grand Prix Changed the World of Formula 1. Red Bull. https://www.redbull.com/sg-en/history-of-the-singapore-grand-prix

The Straits Times. (2020). Covid-19: Tracking the global race to vaccinate. https://www.straitstimes.com/multimedia/graphics/2021/02/covid-vaccine-rollout/index.html?shell

Remembering Lee Kuan Yew. (n.d.). Singapore is out. https://www.remembering.gov.sg/life-and-contributions/mr-lee-and-singapore/singapore-is-out/

Davies, Howard. (2019). Will the UK really turn into 'Singapore-on-Thames' after Brexit?. The Guardian. https://www.theguardian.com/business/2019/dec/17/uk-singapore-on-thames-brexit-france

Thread 54

Townsend, Lee. (n.d.). Recognizing Insect Larval Types. University of Kentucky. https://entomology.ca.uky.edu/ef017#:~:text=About%2075%25%20of%20all%20insect,very%20different%20from%20the%20adult.

Consulus. (2021). What would a 'Corporate Vaccine for Resilience' look like?. https://consulus.com/what-would-a-corporate-vaccine-for-resilience-look-like-whitepaper/

Ternström, Peter. (2021). The epic story behind the Ferrari and Lamborghini rivalry. Grandturismo. https://www.granturismoevents.com/story-the-epic-story-behind-the-ferrari-and-lamborghini-rivalry/

Lamborghini Austin. (2022). What was the most expensive Lamborghini ever built. https://www.lamborghiniaustin.com/blog/2022/february/22/what-was-the-most-expensive-lamborghini-ever-built.htm

Thread 55

Lubich, Chiara (1981). Knowing How to Lose. New City London

Ricci, M. (1602). Kunyu wanguo quantu (Map of the Ten Thousand Countries of the Earth). University of Minnesota Libraries, James Ford Bell Library. https://umedia.lib.umn.edu/item/p16022coll251:8823

Rothstein, Edward. (2010). A Big Map That Shrank the World. New York Times. https://www.nytimes.com/2010/01/20/arts/design/20map.html

Yinping, Qi. (2012). The New Clothes of the Missionaries: Reconsidering Matteo Ricci's Change of Clothes and Alexandre Valignani's "Cultural Accommodation Policy. Zhejiang University. http://jscc.ruc.edu.cn/yw/BACKISSUES/Vol27TranslationandInterpretationofuresSpring2012/27IFaYuShuiFeng/3907f4b642034bb4a5614229ebb5e821.htm

Universita di Bologna. (n.d.). Geographical map by Matteo Ricci. https://museospecola.difa.unibo.it/english/car_65.html

Thread 56

Office of Historian. (n.d.). The Collapse of the Soviet Union. https://history.state.gov/milestones/1989-1992/collapse-soviet-union

Schumpete, Joseph. A. (2011). The Entrepreneur: Classic Texts by Joseph A. Schumpete. Stanford University Press

Roma, Elsa. (2023). Here Is Why Taylor Swift Re-Recording Her Albums Is Every Artists Dream. Forbes. https://www.forbes.com/sites/elsaramo/2023/07/10/here-is-why-taylor-swift-re-recording-her-album-is-every-artists-dream/?sh=1e114d6d66a1

Mitra, Mallika. (2024). Swiftonomics: The Economic Influence of Taylor Swift. Investopedia. https://www.investopedia.com/swiftonomics-definition-8601178

Mao, Frances. (2024). Bad blood over Singapore Taylor Swift Eras tour subsidies. BBC. https://www.bbc.com/news/world-asia-68379688

Aniftos, Rania. (2024). Taylor Swift Is Officially a Billionaire. Billboard. https://www.billboard.com/music/music-news/taylor-swift-forbes-billionaires-list-1235647690/

Grammy Awards. (n.d.). Taylor Swift. https://www.grammy.com/artists/taylor-swift/15450

Thread 57

Guglielmo, Connie. (2012). A Steve Jobs Moment That Mattered: Macworld, August 1997. Forbes. https://www.forbes.com/sites/connieguglielmo/2012/10/07/a-steve-jobs-moment-that-mattered-macworld-august-1997/?sh=4add29c63edd

Huddleston Jr., Tom. (2020). Bill Gates calls Apple's first Mac a 'great machine' in this 1983 internal video. CNBC. https://www.cnbc.com/2020/01/29/video-bill-gates-steve-jobs-in-1983-internal-apple-promo-video.html

Greene, Jay. (2011). Steve Jobs and Bill Gates: It's complicated. CBS News. https://www.cbsnews.com/news/steve-jobs-and-bill-gates-its-complicated/

Klerk, Frederik Willem. (2017). FW de Klerk: The Man Who Ended Apartheid, Freed Mandela and Honored His Country. Arizona State University. https://thunderbird.asu.edu/thought-leadership/insights/fw-de-klerk-man-who-ended-apartheid-freed-mandela-and-honored-his

CBS News. (2013). How Mandela tried to heal the wounds of apartheid. https://www.cbsnews.com/news/how-mandela-tried-to-heal-the-wounds-of-apartheid/

Thread 59

Betz, Eric. (2024). The Kármán Line: Where space begins. Astronomy. https://www.astronomy.com/space-exploration/the-karman-line-where-does-space-begin/

Smola, Jennifer. (2015). Pioneering pilot Jerrie Mock lauded for solo triumph in 1964. Dispatch. https://www.dispatch.com/story/news/2015/12/18/pioneering-pilot-jerrie-mock-lauded/23554415007/

Villenuve, Denis. (Director). (2021). Dune [film]. Legendary Pictures

Issacson, Walter. (2023). Elon Musk. Simon & Schuster

Khalaf, Roula. (2009). A Team Obama of all the talents. Financial Times. https://www.ft.com/content/e17d5436-e1aa-11dd-afa0-0000779fd2ac

Thread 62

Virta Ventures. (n.d,), Lessons From The Greats: Charlie Munger. https://www.virtaventures.co/insights/lessons-from-the-greats-charlie-munger

McKay, Adam. (Director). (2015). Big short [film]. Regency Enterprises and Plan B Entertainment

The Economist. (n.d.). The slumps that shaped modern finance. https://www.economist.com/news/essays/21600451-finance-not-merely-prone-crises-it-shaped-them-five-historical-crises-show-how-aspects-today-s-fina

Horowitz, Julia. (2023). What happens when $2 trillion is sucked out of the global economy? It may not be pretty. CNN. https://edition.cnn.com/2023/05/19/economy/quantitative-tightening-global-impact/index.html

Casarella, Francesco. (2023). Why Warren Buffett's 19.8% Annualized Returns Remain Unmatched. Investing. https://www.investing.com/analysis/why-warren-buffetts-198-annualized-returns-remain-unmatched-200639673

Thread 63

Mamoon, Muntassir (2010). Dhaka: Smiriti Bismiritir Nogori. Anannya.

Khan, Pushpita. (2023). A brief history of Dhaka's administrative transformation. Financial Express. https://thefinancialexpress.com.bd/lifestyle/culture/a-brief-history-of-dhakas-administrative-transformation

Khandker, Hissam. (2015). Which India is claiming to have been colonised?. The Daily Star. https://www.thedailystar.net/op-ed/politics/which-india-claiming-have-been-colonised-119284

The World Bank. (2018). Bangladesh: Reducing Poverty and Sharing Prosperity. https://www.worldbank.org/en/results/2018/11/15/bangladesh-reducing-poverty-and-sharing-prosperity

House, Frances. (2012). The Dhaka Principles for Migration With Dignity. Institute for Human Rights and Business. https://www.ihrb.org/focus-areas/migrant-workers/commentary-dhaka-principles-migration-dignity

Consulus. (2012). Changing the World through Marketing – World Marketing Summit 2012. https://consulus.com/changing-the-world-through-marketing-world-marketing-summit-2012/

Thread 64

Kurlantzick, Joshua. (2011). After Deng: On China's Transformation. The Nation. https://www.thenation.com/article/archive/after-deng-chinas-transformation/

Denmark, Abraham. (2018). 40 years ago, Deng Xiaoping changed China — and the world. Washington Post. https://www.washingtonpost.com/news/monkey-cage/wp/2018/12/19/40-years-ago-deng-xiaoping-changed-china-and-the-world/

National University of Singapore. (n.d.). Building on Deng Xiaoping and Lee Kuan Yew Legacy: Today Marks 40th Anniversary of Deng's Historic Visit to Singapore. https://cil.nus.edu.sg/publication/building-on-deng-xiaoping-and-lee-kuan-yew-legacy-today-marks-40th-anniversary-of-dengs-historic-visit-to-singapore/

The World Bank. (n.d.). The World Bank in China. https://www.worldbank.org/en/country/china/overview

The World Bank. (n.d.). Lifting 800 Million People Out of Poverty – New Report Looks at Lessons from China's Experience. https://www.worldbank.org/en/news/press-release/2022/04/01/lifting-800-million-people-out-of-poverty-new-report-looks-at-lessons-from-china-s-experience

Thread 65

People's Daily Online. (2024). China's operating high-speed railway hits 45,000 km. http://en.people.cn/n3/2024/0109/c90000-20119756.html

NPR. (2024). Construction has begun on the first American high speed rail system. https://www.npr.org/2024/04/23/1246546154/construction-has-begun-on-the-first-american-high-speed-rail-system#

Mooallem, Jon. (2019). Train Across America. The New York Times Magazine. https://www.nytimes.com/interactive/2019/03/20/magazine/train-across-america-amtrak.html

Ohnsman, Alan. (2023). 'The Greenest Bullet Train In The World': Wes Edens   Wants To Kickstart U.S. High-Speed Rail With A Vegas-L.A. Line. Forbes. https://www.forbes.com/sites/alanohnsman/2023/04/25/the-greenest-bullet-train-in-the-world-wes-edens-wants-to-kickstart-us-high-speed-rail-with-a-vegas-la-line/?sh=559d0d7f630b

Association of American Railroads. (n.d.) Chronology of America's Freight Railroads. https://www.aar.org/chronology-of-americas-freight-railroads/

Crawford, Krysten. (2024). Nvidia's Jensen Huang: The incredible future of AI. Stanford. https://siepr.stanford.edu/news/nvidias-jensen-huang-incredible-future-ai

Companies Market Cap. (n.d.). NVIDIA. https://companiesmarketcap.com/nvidia/marketcap/

Thread 66

Haden, Jeff. (2023). Elon Musk's 'Algorithm,' a 5-Step Process to Dramatically Improve Nearly Anything, Is Both Simple and Brilliant. Inc. https://www.inc.com/jeff-haden/elon-musks-algorithm-a-5-step-process-to-dramatically-improve-nearly-everything-is-both-simple-brilliant.html

Thread 67

Vatican. (n.d.). Biography of POPE JOHN XXIII 1958-1963. https://www.vatican.va/content/john-xxiii/en/biography/documents/hf_j-xxiii_bio_16071997_biography.html

BBC. (2013). Conclave: How cardinals elect a Pope. https://www.bbc.com/news/world-21412589

Whitehead, Kenneth D. (2012). Fifty Years of Vatican II. Catholic. https://www.catholic.com/magazine/print-edition/fifty-years-of-vatican-ii

Ratcliffe, Susan. (2017). Oxford Essential Quotations (5 ed.). Oxford University Press.

Solzhentitsyn, Alexsandr. (n.d.). Communism and Religion. Victims of Communism. https://victimsofcommunism.org/curriculum-chapter-3/

Bernstein, Richard. (2005). Pope helped bring Poland its freedom. New York Times. https://www.nytimes.com/2005/04/06/world/europe/pope-helped-bring-poland-its-freedom.html

Thread 68

Clifford, Catherine. (2018). What Warren Buffett taught Bill Gates about managing time by sharing his (nearly) blank calendar. CNBC. https://www.cnbc.com/2018/09/07/warren-buffett-taught-bill-gates-about-time-management-by-sharing-his-blank-calendar.html

Thread 70

Consulus. (2021). What would a 'Corporate Vaccine for Resilience' look like?. https://consulus.com/what-would-a-corporate-vaccine-for-resilience-look-like-whitepaper/

Thread 71

Ramthun, Jake & Mishra, Vikalp. (2022). Lunar Landscaping: How Digging 'Half-Moons' Helps Re-Green Niger. Climatelinks. https://www.climatelinks.org/blog/lunar-landscaping-how-digging-half-moons-helps-re-green-niger

Blakemore, Erin. (2019). What was the Neolithic Revolution?. National Geographic. https://www.nationalgeographic.com/culture/article/neolithic-agricultural-revolution

World Food Programme. (n.d.). A global food crisis. (n.d.). https://www.wfp.org/global-hunger-crisis

Statista. (n.d.). Food - Worldwide. https://www.statista.com/outlook/cmo/food/worldwide#revenue

AG Funder. (2023). AgFunder Global AgriFoodTech Investment Report 2023. https://agfunder.com/research/agfunder-global-agrifoodtech-investment-report-2023/

Good Food Institute. (n.d.). Investing in alternative protein. https://gfi.org/investment/

NASA. (n.d.). Growing Plants in Space. https://www.nasa.gov/exploration-research-and-technology/growing-plants-in-space/

Thread 72

CIGRE. (n.d.). The electric power system in East Malaysia, Sarawak. https://www.cigre.org/userfiles/files/Community/National%20Power%20System/CIGRE_Information_on_National_Power_Systems_EastMalaysia_Sarawak_V2.pdf

Gin, Ooi Keat & Seng, Vincent Lim Choon. (n.d.). Sarawak's economy from the late 19th century to the mid-20th century. Economic History of Malaya. https://www.ehm.my/publications/articles/sarawaks-economy-from-the-late-19th-century-to-the-mid-20th-century

Aubrey, Samuel. (2023). Premier: State's commitment to sustainable devt attracting global attention, investments. The Borneo Post. https://www.theborneopost.com/2023/12/06/premier-states-commitment-to-sustainable-devt-attracting-global-attention-investments/

Ming, Lau Chai. (2023). Mainstreaming biodiversity in Malaysia through UNDP and Sarawak's collaboration. UNDP. https://www.undp.org/malaysia/blog/mainstreaming-biodiversity-malaysia-through-undp-and-sarawaks-collaboration#

Lee, Chermaine. (2023). COP28 Deal a 'Disappointing' Win, Experts and Activists Say. Voa News. https://www.voanews.com/a/cop28-deal-a-disappointing-win-experts-and-activists-say-/7396512.html

Ikeda, Satoshi & Glynn, Simon. (2023). Economic Incentives Are Key to Driving Sustainability at Scale. MIT Sloan Management Review. https://sloanreview.mit.edu/article/economic-incentives-are-key-to-driving-sustainability-at-scale/

Cullen, Art. (2020). The US is headed for climate disaster – but Joe Biden's green plan might just work. The Guardian. https://www.theguardian.com/commentisfree/2020/jul/16/joe-biden-green-plan-democrats-climate-crisis

BloombergNef. (2022). Global Investment in Low-Carbon Energy Transition Hit $755 Billion in 2021. https://about.bnef.com/blog/global-investment-in-low-carbon-energy-transition-hit-755-billion-in-2021/

Jean, Francois Bastin et al. (2019). The global tree restoration potential. Science365, 76-79. DOI:10.1126/science.aax0848

Kilgore, Georgette. (2023). How Many Trees Are Planted Each Year? Full List By Country, Type, Year. 8 Billion Trees. https://8billiontrees.com/trees/how-many-trees-are-planted-each-year/

World Economic Forum. (2024). Investing in trees: global companies are protecting and restoring forests. https://www.weforum.org/impact/investing-in-trees/

Thread 73

Jones, Rachyl. (2024). What the AI revolt in the 'Dune' universe warns us about today. Fortune. https://fortune.com/2024/03/08/dune-ai-warning/

Matthews, Dylan. (2023). 40 years ago   today, one man saved us from world-ending nuclear war. Vox. https://www.vox.com/2018/9/26/17905796/nuclear-war-1983-stanislav-petrov-soviet-union

Kemp, Simon. (2024). Digital 2023: Global Overview Report. Data Reportal. https://datareportal.com/reports/digital-2023-global-overview-report

The Business Research Company. (2024). Social Media Global Market Report 2024. https://www.researchandmarkets.com/report/social-media

Bremmer, Ian. (2023). The Next Global Superpower Isn't Who You Think. TED. https://www.ted.com/talks/ian_bremmer_the_next_global_superpower_isn_t_who_you_think?language=en

Bloomberg. (2023). Generative AI races toward $1.3 trillion in revenue by 2032. https://www.bloomberg.com/professional/insights/data/generative-ai-races-toward-1-3-trillion-in-revenue-by-2032

Thread 74

Sengupta, Arjun. (2023). Remembering Mangalyaan: How ISRO's Mars Orbiter Mission was a great leap for India. Indiana Express. https://indianexpress.com/article/explained/explained-sci-tech/mangalyaan-mars-orbiter-mission-8954001/

McKinsey. (2023). A giant leap for the space industry. https://www.mckinsey.com/featured-insights/sustainable-inclusive-growth/chart-of-the-day/a-giant-leap-for-the-space-industry

Sheetz, Michael. (2023). SpaceX valuation climbs to $180 billion. CNBC. https://www.cnbc.com/2023/12/13/spacex-value-climbs-to-180-billion-higher-than-boeing-verizon.html

Davidson, Helen. (2024). The new 'space race': what are China's ambitions and why is the US so concerned. The Guardian. https://www.theguardian.com/world/article/2024/may/05/the-new-space-race-what-are-chinas-ambitions-and-why-is-the-us-so-concerned

Fleming, Maxwell. (2023). Mining in space could spur sustainable growth. Proceedings of the National Academy of Sciences of the United States of America. https://www.pnas.org/doi/10.1073/pnas.2221345120

Thread 75

Bible Gateway. (n.d.). Four Horsemen of the Apocalypse. (n.d.). https://www.biblegateway.com/passage/?search=Revelation%206&version=TLV

Thread 76

Bolinger, Hope. (2024). What was the Tower of Babel?. Christianity. https://www.christianity.com/wiki/christian-terms/what-was-the-tower-of-babel.html

Piazza, James. (2020). Politician hate speech and domestic terrorism. Research Gate. https://www.researchgate.net/publication/340275440_Politician_hate_speech_and_domestic_terrorism

Vatican. (2019). Document for Human Fraternity for World Peace and Living Together. https://www.vatican.va/content/francesco/en/travels/2019/outside/documents/papa-francesco_20190204_documento-fratellanza-umana.html

Religion for Peace. (n.d.). Ring for Peace. https://www.rfp.org/wp-content/uploads/2020/10/rfp-info-ringforpeace-en3.pdf

Thread 77

Dilanian, Ken & Ainsley, Julia. (2021). What went wrong with security at the Capitol?. NBC News. https://www.nbcnews.com/news/crime-courts/what-went-wrong-security-capitol-n1253341

Venkataramakrishnan, Siddharth. (2023). How digital cash got caught up in the culture wars. Financial Times. https://www.ft.com/content/ab8fbe73-34bf-4624-b394-97f995551f7a

Lamb, Stefanie. (2005). Introduction to the Cultural Revolution. Stanford Program on International and Cross-Cultural Education. https://spice.fsi.stanford.edu/docs/introduction_to_the_cultural_revolution

Jones, Jeffrey M. (2023). Americans Trust Local Government Most, Congress Least. Gallup. Retrieved from https://news.gallup.com

Denning, Steve. (2014). Making Sense Of Zappos And Holacracy. Forbes. https://www.forbes.com/sites/stevedenning/2014/01/15/making-sense-of-zappos-and-holacracy/?sh=7f08606d3207

Synod. (n.d.). Pope Francis and the Synodal Process. https://www.synod.va/en/resources/pope-francis-and-the-synodal-process.html

Lee, Kuan Yew. (1984). Speech by Prime Minister on the Second Reading of the Constitution of the Republic of Singapore Bill in Parliament. NAS. https://www.nas.gov.sg/archivesonline/data/pdfdoc/lky19840724.pdf

Thread 78

Cox, Jeff. (2023). Jamie Dimon lashes out against crypto: 'If I was the government, I'd close it down'. CNBC. https://www.cnbc.com/2023/12/06/jamie-dimon-lashes-out-on-crypto-if-i-was-the-government-id-close-it-down.html

Shin, Hyun Song. (2022). The great crypto crisis is upon us. Bank for International Settlements. https://www.bis.org/speeches/sp221216.htm

Sigalos, Mackenzie. (2024). From 25 years in prison to just four months: Inside the final verdict on a crypto billionaire CEO archrivalry. CNBC. https://www.cnbc.com/2024/05/05/inside-the-final-prison-verdict-on-an-epic-crypto-ceo-rivalry.html

Lee, Yen Nee. (2017). India tried to get the 'black money' out of its banking system — it ended up doing the opposite. CNBC. https://www.cnbc.com/2017/09/07/demonetization-reserve-bank-of-india-suggests-that-demonetisation-allowed-black-money-to-enter-banking-system.html

Sachs, Jeffrey D. (2021). Time to Overhaul the Global Financial System. Center for International Relations and Sustainable Development. https://www.cirsd.org/en/cirsd-recommends/time-to-overhaul-the-global-financial-system

Economy of Communion. (n.d.). What is the EOC?. https://eocnoam.org/what-is-the-eoc/

Thread 79

Grand View Research. (2023). Higher Education Market Size & Trends. Rhttps://www.grandviewresearch.com/industry-analysis/higher-education-market

Global Times. (2024). China's youth unemployment rate remains flat in March at 15.3%. https://www.globaltimes.cn/page/202404/1310845.shtml

Umoh, Ruth. (2018). Richard Branson says the 3 skills all successful CEOs need are not taught in schools. CNBC. https://www.cnbc.com/2018/01/17/richard-branson-says-the-3-skills-ceos-need-are-not-taught-in-schools.html

Hetzner, Christiaan. (2024). Elon Musk blasts obsolete education system for failing to reach kids: 'You don't want a teacher in front of a board'. Fortune. https://fortune.com/2024/05/07/elon-musk-tesla-education-teaching-interactive-entertainment-children/

6 Sense. (n.d.). Top 5 Learning Management Systems technologies in 2024

https://6sense.com/tech/learning-management-systems